BOWHUNTING THE WHITETAIL DEER

BOWHUNTING THE WHITETAIL DEER

DEAN CONATSER

Winchester Press

Library of Congress Cataloging in Publication Data

Conatser, Dean.
    Bowhunting the whitetail deer.

    Includes index.
    1. Hunting with bow and arrow. 2. White-tailed deer hunting. I. Title.
SK36.C65   799.2′0285   77-23244
ISBN 0-87691-192-0

Published by Winchester Press
205 East 42nd Street
New York, N.Y. 10017

Winchester is a Trademark of Olin Corporation used
by Winchester Press, Inc., under authority and control
of the Trademark Proprietor.

Printed in the United States of America

To my grandfather and father from whom I inherited my love for hunting and to my four children, Reneé, Timothy, Drew, and Amber, one or all of whom I hope carries on the tradition.

CONTENTS

Contents

PREFACE

Up until a few years ago, when most people heard the words "bow and arrow," they thought of Robin Hood and Sherwood Forest, the American Indians and buffalo hunts, or pygmies and Africa. Most of them would have laughed had they been told that archery can be an exciting sport and an extremely challenging way to hunt. However, in more recent years, thanks to men like Howard Hill, Fred Bear, Art Young, and Saxton Pope, just to mention a few, archery has become one of America's favorite sports, a form of recreation that the whole family can enjoy.

Every year more and more people are picking up a bow and trying to shoot an arrow into a target. Many of these beginners are non-hunters and want to shoot a bow for pleasure or for the competition it offers through local, state, and national archery clubs. These people usually become target archers. They shoot at known distances, use light bows, light arrows, string releases, sights, stabilizers, and any other means considered legal to help them put five arrows into a spot the size of a quarter. Archery in itself is enough sport for these people and they could not care less about hunting with a bow.

Other beginners are hunters, old hands as well as neo-phytes, and they want to use a bow and arrow to bag game. Many of them are experienced rifle hunters who do not get the same thrill they once did when they drop a deer at 200 yards using a high-powered rifle and scope, so they want to face the challenge of "trying" to bag a deer at less than 40 yards with a bow and arrow. For them this is a real feat.

Still other prospective bowhunters have never hunted deer at all. My wife, for example, looks forward to bowhunting each year, but will not even consider hunting with a rifle. She feels that there is no challenge if the deer can be dropped 150 or 200 yards away. To her, the challenge is having to get up close.

When using a primitive weapon like the bow and arrow for hunting, it takes more than just the ability to shoot to be able to bag game such as the whitetail deer. The bowhunter must also be an accomplished woodsman. He must know the habits of the deer, the art of camouflage, the way to control odors. He must be patient. He must be able to go home at the end of the season without a deer and still say that he enjoyed the hunt, because the success ratio of bowhunters when compared to rifle hunters is very low. Most real bowhunters just enjoy being in the woods as much as the actual taking of a deer. Bagging one only adds frosting to the cake.

The beginning bowhunters are the archers to whom this guide is addressed. They know very little or nothing about archery and many of them know even less about hunting. By reading this guide those beginners may be able to avoid some of the problems of trial and error that most bowhunters have been through.

Although this guide is about bowhunting, it will not cover the history of the bow and arrow. Such history would make wonderful reading for a bowhunter, but it wouldn't help him very much in the deer woods. There are many good books available that are written by experts on the history of archery with detailed descriptions of all types of bows, from those used by ancient man to the present, and I recommend those volumes to the person interested in all aspects of archery.

Preface

In this guide target archery will be discussed only in order to make comparisons with bowhunting. That is not to say that target archery is not an exciting sport, because it is, but the equipment, style, and intent for target archery are completely dissimilar to those of bowhunting, so to discuss both sports in detail would confuse the beginning bowhunter.

The purpose of this guide is to provide the information needed by beginners who plan to hunt with their bows, and also to add a little knowledge to the skills of the experienced bowhunters. After reading and studying this guide, there is no guarantee that a beginner will be able to go into the woods and kill a whitetail deer with ease, or even at all, but at least he will be better prepared to meet that enormous challenge.

PART I

CHOICE
OF
EQUIPMENT

The most important items on the list of equipment for bow-hunting are, of course, the bow and the arrows. These should be chosen with care and with help from a competent archery dealer, if at all possible. Many discount houses, pawn shops, and garage auctions have bows for sale, but these are not the places for a beginner to buy his first bow. Of course, he can find a cheap bow there, but when he gets home and starts trying to shoot, he will very quickly realize that he should have gone to an archery dealer.

I had been a rifle hunter for years when I finally got the urge to try the bow and arrow. I went to a local discount store and found exactly what I thought I wanted. It was a 68-pound re-curve bow, 62 inches long, and when I asked the store sales-man if it would be a good bow for deer hunting, he did not know. He had been transferred to the sporting-goods depart-ment from ladies' wear the week before, and had never hunted a day in his life. That is one of the problems a beginner may run into when buying a bow in a place where the clerks are inexperienced in archery and hunting.

I finally decided that the bow was what I needed, and I pur-chased it. When I got home, my problems began. I had never strung a recurve bow and there were no instructions with the one I had purchased. After searching through sev-eral outdoor books, I found an article on the bow and arrow and read how to string a bow—but I never did get it strung.

The next day I took my new bow and the "fifty-cent spe-cial" arrows that I had bought to a friend who had been an archer for several years. After his laughter had subsided and he'd grown tired of poking fun at me, he explained what I had done and what I should do if I really wanted to become an archer.

Now that I have been an archer and bowhunter for several years, I can appreciate my friend telling me that day that I should hang my new bow on the wall for decoration and use the arrows to kindle a fire. The bow was much too powerful for a beginner, or for most experienced archers for that matter, and even if I had succeeded in getting it strung, I would probably not have been able to draw it, much less shoot it. Also, the arrows were of such low quality that a 68-pound bow could have very easily broken one of them and sent it through my forearm rather than at a target.

The following is what I *should* have done.

THE BOW

Many writers recommend that a beginning archer buy a cheap bow to find out if he really wants to become a bow-hunter before he spends a large sum of money. This is sound advice only if the beginner goes to a qualified dealer to buy that cheap bow. By "cheap," I do not mean a bow a person would buy his children to play with, but a good inexpensive bow. There are several on the market that will not upset your bank account too much, or you can buy a good used bow if you prefer. In my opinion, the used bow is best, because you can find many used bows that are of good quality, yet cost no more than a poorer quality new bow. As long as the bow is not cracked or warped, it doesn't really matter if you are not the first owner. The main thing is to choose a bow that you can shoot.

The following chart will give you an idea of what pound bow you should buy. "Pound" does not refer to the actual weight of the bow, but to the amount of energy required to draw the bow to 28 inches (the standard draw length for measuring bow weight in pounds).

Young children	10–15 pounds
Ten to twelve years	15–20 pounds
Teen-age girls and women	20–30 pounds
Teen-age boys and men	30–40 pounds
Men's hunting bows	40–55 pounds

Keep in mind that this chart is only a guideline since some people are naturally stronger than others and will shoot heavier bows. Also, target archers will use much lighter bows than hunting archers.

Many men and some women try to shoot bows that are much too heavy for them, because they feel that it is a sign of weakness to shoot a lighter bow. Do not make that mistake. After shooting a lighter bow for a while, the muscles required for shooting will strengthen and an archer will be able to work up to a heavier bow if he so desires.

Many archery "experts" recommend that a person buy two identical bows except in weight; a light bow somewhere in the 33- to 38-pound range for learning to shoot and for practice, and a heavy bow, 40 to 55 pounds, for hunting. This is a good method if the person can afford it. But be sure to start practicing with the heavier bow well in advance of hunting season. The greater strength of the heavier bow will cause the arrow to fly differently than arrows shot from the lighter bow, even though the two are identical except in weight. I have known hunters who did all of their preseason practice with a light bow then expected to hit a deer on opening morning with a heavy bow. Needless to say, the success ratio was low. This would be like a gun hunter using a .22 rifle for practice then switching to a .30/06 for deer season without ever having shot the larger magnum gun before. Also, arrows spined for a 45-pound bow will be too heavy for a 35-pound bow and will have a tendency to drop much faster, so the archer will need a set of arrows spined for each bow. (See the section on arrows for a more detailed discussion of arrow spine and bow weight.)

Beginning bowhunters should also check with the game commission of their state to see if there is a minimum bow-weight requirement for bowhunting. Many states require that a bow be able to cast an arrow tipped with a hunting point for a certain number of yards (usually 125 yards) before deer or larger game may be hunted. This is not a bad requirement since the bow must be strong enough to cause the arrow to penetrate into the vital organs of an animal. There are cases of deer being taken with 30-pound bows, but here again the success ratio is limited.

A weight range from 42 pounds up to 56 pounds is strong enough for whitetail deer, yet light enough for the average bowhunter. Regardless of the bow weight you choose, be able to shoot it well and your chances for bagging a deer will be greatly increased.

Choice of Equipment

After deciding on the bow weight, the beginner should determine if he needs to shoot a left-handed or right-handed bow. The fact that a person is right-handed does not mean that he will shoot a right-handed bow. The determining factor is the dominant or stronger eye, not the arm or hand (assuming that the beginner has no physical problems with his limbs).

Both eyes open

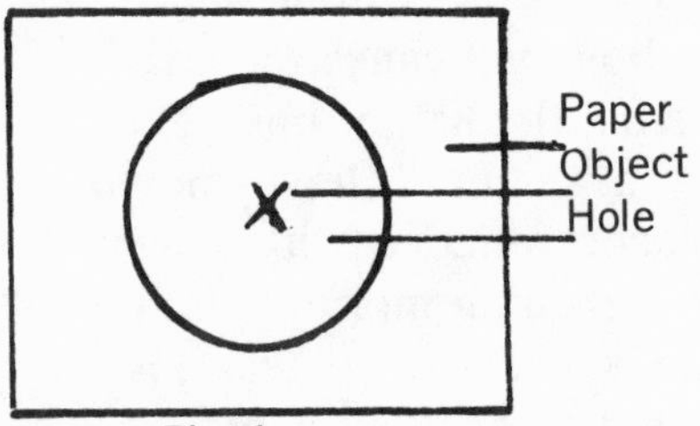

Right eye open,
left eye closed

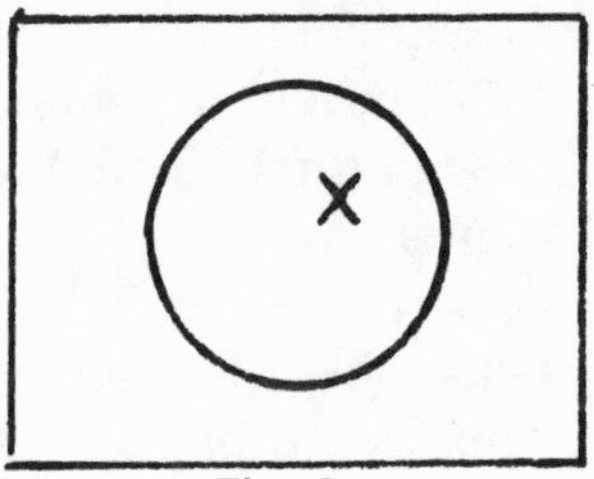

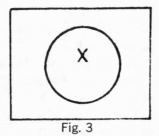

Paper
Object
Hole

Fig. 1

Fig. 2

Left eye open,
right eye closed

Fig. 3

To determine which eye is dominant, take a small square of paper and cut or tear a hole in the center of it about the size of a dime. With both arms extended straight in front of the body, hold the square of paper with the thumbs and forefingers of both hands. With both eyes open, look through the small hole and focus on some distant object (Fig. 1). Close the left eye. If the object is still in focus through the hole, the right eye is dominant (Fig. 2). If the object is not in focus with the left eye closed, close the right eye and open the left eye. The left eye is dominant if the object is then in focus through the hole (Fig. 3).

Many beginning archers refuse to change hands for shooting a bow even though their "off-hand" eye is dominant. They do not feel comfortable trying to pull a bow "cross-handed" as they sometimes call it. However, when first learning to shoot a bow, it is difficult to draw a bow with either hand, so start out in the correct way and a lot of future problems may be avoided. Many right-handed archers shoot left-handed and vice versa.

There are three major types of bows for an archer to choose from: the straight or longbow, the recurve bow, and the compound bow. Some archers consider the takedown bow as a fourth type, but the majority of these bows are take-apart versions of the straight or the recurve bow.

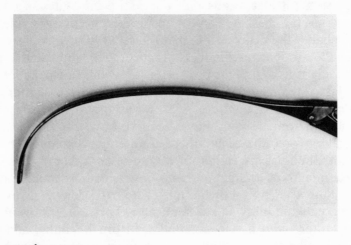

Recurve bow.

Straight and Recurve Bows

As seen in the above photo, the limb tips curve away from the archer when the recurve bow is held in the shooting position. The limb tips are straight or bend slightly toward the archer on a straight bow.

One of America's most famous archers, Howard Hill, used a straight bow to perform some amazing feats and to kill some of the world's most feared animals. On the other hand, an equally famous American archer and manufacturer of archery equipment, Fred Bear, has used a recurve bow to perform equally amazing feats and to kill an equally impressive number of the world's most feared animals, so who can really say which design, straight or recurve, is the best?

Both the straight and recurve designs have their advantages and their disadvantages. Howard Hill once said that he was not good enough to shoot a recurve bow. By that he meant that the recurve bow has a tendency to overemphasize minor shooting errors, thus making them more difficult to shoot with accuracy. The recurve bow is such a popular design today that it is difficult even to find a good straight bow anymore. This is not to say that a good straight bow is not a fine piece of equipment; it just means that popularity and sales of equipment rule the market, and the recurve is the present ruler.

Probably the main reason that the recurve bow is preferred over the straight bow is that a recurve with the same length and weight as a straight bow is easier to draw, stacks less in the last few inches of draw, and casts the arrow flatter and faster than the straight bow. So for all practical purposes, a beginning archer should buy a recurve bow when he decides to make his purchase, and there are literally dozens of styles, lengths, and draw weights for him to choose from.

The length of a target archer's bow is usually much longer than that used by a bowhunter. The extra length gives the bow greater stability and easier draw. The shorter bow of the bowhunter, who has to contend with brush, limbs, and the like when he shoots, allows better maneuverability when he is trying to get into a position to shoot at a deer through heavy brush or out of a tree.

Most modern bows are laminated fiberglass and hardwood. This means that two strips of fiberglass with a strip of hardwood are bonded together with resin in such a way that they can withstand the stress and strain required for shooting an arrow. Most manufacturers have adopted this bonded combination for their best bows. There are still a few wood bows and solid fiberglass bows available, but they are usually in the less expensive range.

The Takedown Bow

When a takedown bow is assembled, it looks just like any other bow. The only difference is that it can be broken down into two or three pieces for easier storage and transporting. The takedown design is not a new concept; it has been around for many years. Just thumb through an archery catalog and note how many different designs there are on the market.

One popular design comes apart in the middle of the handle and is held in place by milled grooves and a long screw. Another design has three pieces with each limb being held to the middle section by a screw. Still another and highly effective design incorporates strong clips to hold the limbs onto the middle section.

One great asset of the three-part bow is the replacement of warped or broken limbs without having to buy a complete new bow. Also, limbs are interchangeable. With a set of light limbs and a set of heavy limbs, by simply changing the limbs the archer can have two bows in one, a light bow for practice and target shooting and a heavier bow for hunting.

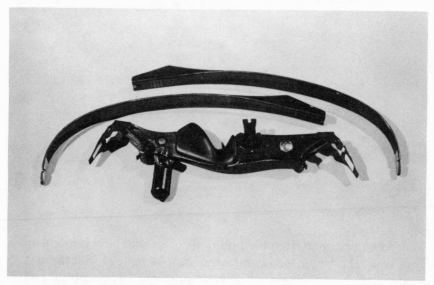

Three-piece takedown bow.

The Compound Bow

The compound bow is one of the most controversial bow designs ever to hit the archery market. Many proponents of the more classical longbow and recurve bow contend that the compound is a mechanical device much like the crossbow and it should not be legal for either competitive archery or bow-hunting. On the other hand, proponents of the compound believe that it should be classified as a bow since it is drawn like a bow, aimed like a bow, and released like a bow, and it should be legal wherever bows are used. The compound bow has both advantages and disadvantages in the deer woods. Only after the bowhunter becomes familiar with the compound can he decide for himself whether he wants to use it or one of the more traditional designs.

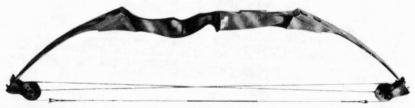

Compound bow.

As can be seen from the photo, a compound bow is made up of several crisscrossed cables and various pulleys, but there is also the basic design of a bow present. The cables and pulleys allow the compound to shoot much faster and with a flatter trajectory than a traditional bow of the same draw weight.

The break-over feature of the compound bow is its greatest advantage over other bows. For example, a 50-pound draw weight will break over at about two-thirds full draw, due to the cam action of the pulleys, to approximately 30 to 35 pounds. In other words, the archer will be holding 30 to 35 pounds at full draw, then when he releases the arrow it is catapulted from the bow at 50 pounds. This allows the archer to hold and aim with a low draw weight and he will have less tendency to snap shoot. He may thus shoot a heavy bow with the ease of a lighter one.

When the arrow is released on a traditional bow, it immediately begins to lose velocity even before it clears the shot window. However, when an arrow is released on a compound bow the greatest amount of thrust is not reached until the arrow passes the break-over point at which time the velocity is actually increased by the same cam action that allowed the bow to break over to a lower full draw weight. This extra velocity creates flatter trajectory, faster speed, and deeper penetration.

Although the compound has several advantages over traditional bows, it also has several disadvantages. The actual weight of a compound is much heavier than other bows, which causes more fatigue on the hunter when he is carrying it on a long hunt or practicing for long periods of time. Also, due to the many cables, twigs and leaves are frequently snagged and caught as the hunter walks through heavy brush. Another bad feature of the compound is the process of changing a string, which requires several steps before it can be accomplished.

I am sure that in an argument between a proponent and an opponent of the compound, several other advantages and disadvantages would be discussed. If an archer is interested in a compound bow, he should go to an archery shop, look at one, shoot it, and evaluate it himself. Then, if he chooses to buy one and can kill a deer with it, the compound is the bow for him.

PARTS OF A BOW

Most archers have either read or heard tales where some bowhunter broke a bowstring during a deer hunt and did not have a replacement with him. Out of necessity he used a shoe lace or a strip of leather for a string and killed a big buck. That would really be a feat to remember and to tell grandchildren, but the chances of success are few and far between.

The Bowstring

The bowstring is as important to accurate shooting as any other part of the bow, and like the arrows, it should be matched to the bow. A 62-inch string should not be used on a 64-inch bow, nor is it practical or safe to use a string made for a 35-pound bow on a 50-pound bow. There are strings made for every length and bow weight, so finding the correct string is not hard.

The advanced bowhunter may even choose to make his own bowstring. This isn't too difficult with a few proper steps and tools. However, the beginner should buy his strings at an archery shop to ensure proper length and weight.

There are loops (eyes) at each end of the string, which fit over the tips of the bow. One loop is larger than the other. The reason for this will be explained in the section on "bracing" or stringing the bow. Note that approximately in the middle of the string (at pencil point) there is a wrapped area. This is the "serving," and the purpose of the extra wrapping is to cut down on string wear, since this is the part of the string where the arrow is nocked and where the fingers make contact, thus causing more wear. Each end of the string is also wrapped in the same manner.

The Nocking Point

The nocking point is not on the string when it is purchased. It must be added later by the archer. Its purpose is to allow the archer to place the arrow on the string at exactly the same spot every time. This is important for consistent shooting, since an arrow that is nocked high will strike the target lower than one that is nocked low.

Some archers prefer to use a mark on the serving rather than a nocking point. This is fine except that under hunting conditions, it is sometimes difficult to keep a watch on a deer and look for the mark on the string at the same time. By using a nocking point, the archer can slip an arrow on the string, then simply move it up or down the string until it stops at the nocking point. It is then in proper position for shooting.

Other archers prefer to use two nocking points, one above and one below the arrow. However, like the mark on the string, it is sometimes difficult to place the arrow between the two nocking points under hunting conditions.

Bowstrings are easily cut by sharp objects and they do wear out from shooting, so a smart hunter will take at least one spare with him on every hunting trip. The spare should be used several times prior to the hunting trip to get rid of the stretch that occurs in a new bowstring. This stretching can cause the nocking point to change and the archer will shoot too high or too low.

Until modern times, bowstrings were made from linen whereas most of today's strings are made from Dacron. The weight of the bow they are designed for determines the number of strands to be used in each string. For example, a heavier bow will need a string with more strands than a lighter bow will require. A qualified archery dealer is able to provide the exact string needed for each bow.

Never use a worn string. If it should break while the archer is shooting, the bow or the archer, or perhaps both, may be hurt severely.

Arrow Rest

The arrow rest is a device that fits to the side of the bow just above or on the bow shelf. Its purpose is to hold the arrow above the bow shelf to prevent the bottom feather from coming in contact with the shelf and causing the arrow to buck up as it is shot.

There are many different designs and materials used for arrow rests, but the hunting archer should choose one that allows the arrow to be drawn with the least amount of friction noise. Believe me, a deer can hear an arrow being drawn across the arrow rest if it is within 10 or 15 yards of the hunter. Plastic or metal designs are great for target archery where noise is of no concern, but the serious deer hunter should use either a feather rest or one made from soft leather.

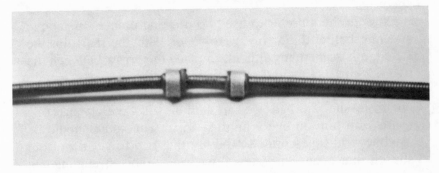

Nocking point.

Another good way to eliminate friction noise as the arrow is drawn across the arrow rest is to coat the arrow with wax. This will also dull the finish of the arrow, which helps to cut down on glare.

THE ARROWS

Some archers believe that with a good arrow, any stick and string will serve for a bow. That may be going a little too far, but as long as the arrows are straight and of good quality they will shoot fairly well from just about any bow they match.

Most sporting-goods stores carry ready-made arrows in lengths from 24 to 30 inches already fitted with a tip. This is fine if the archer knows his draw length (the distance he draws a bow), the spine or stiffness of the arrows he needs, and if the arrows are tipped with the type of point he wants. However, everyone does not have the same draw length, shoot the same weight bow, or want the same type points, and the beginner especially does not know what he wants or needs. So he should go to a qualified archery dealer, if at all possible, to purchase his first set of arrows.

An archery dealer will be able to measure the draw length of the archer, check the bow weight, choose the proper arrow spine needed, and then cut the arrows to the exact length required for each individual archer. Also, the archer will be able to choose the type of point he wants and even the color of the fletching (feathers). This kind of service is just not available in a sporting-goods store.

Length

The proper arrow length is very important. For example, an arrow that is too long does not fly as well as it should. It has a tendency to drop too soon due to the extra weight, which will cause the archer to get into the habit of aiming too high. An arrow that is too short may be overdrawn by the archer. This is very dangerous, because an overdrawn arrow will fall behind the bow shelf and when released may go through the archer's hand or forearm or hit someone else who may be standing nearby.

There are many practical ways to measure the draw length but probably the best and most accurate is to use a lightweight bow (20 to 25 pounds for adults and 10 to 15 pounds for children) and a very long arrow. Draw the arrow as if it were going to be shot and bring it all the way back to the anchor point (anchor point is discussed in the section on how to shoot). Hold the draw and have another person mark the arrow with a pencil at the point where it crosses the front of the bow. Repeat this procedure several times to be sure that the draw is made to the same place each time. Measure the arrow from the pencil mark to the nock, and that is the correct arrow length needed. Most dealers have arrows made up with premeasured marks already on them, which makes measuring the draw length easier and more accurate.

Another good method used to measure draw length is to have someone measure the distance from fingertips to fingertips of the archer's outspread arms. Then, by using the following chart, the correct arrow length may be determined.

Measure from fingertips to fingertips

Spread measurement	Arrow length
57–59 inches	24–25 inches
60–62 inches	25–26 inches
63–65 inches	26–27 inches
66–68 inches	27–28 inches
69–71 inches	28–29 inches
72–74 inches	29–30 inches
75–77 inches	30–31 inches

Arrows for beginners and children should always be cut approximately ½ inch longer, because the draw of a new archer may lengthen as he becomes more used to shooting. After proper form has been developed, arrows can be cut to exact length.

After the arrow length is established, the archer needs to decide which type of arrow he wants to shoot. There are three major materials used for arrow shafts on the market today: wood, fiberglass, and aluminum. Each material has its advantages and its shortcomings, so the archer should consider his own personal needs before purchasing one of them. Most archers try all three before finally deciding which is best for his particular type of hunting.

Wood Arrows

Wood shafts are the most practical for the beginning archer. They are much cheaper than fiberglass or aluminum, and until the beginner learns to shoot where he aims, he will lose and break a few arrows, so there's little point in his buying more expensive arrows while learning. Wood arrows do have a tendency to warp if they aren't handled properly. They can be straightened by holding them over a pot of boiling water for a few minutes, then applying pressure with both hands to hold them in shape until they cool. Continue this procedure until they are straight.

Do not bend arrows too much or they will warp in the other direction. After a little practice, a feel for the proper amount of pressure will be developed.

Fiberglass Arrows

Fiberglass arrows fall in the middle price range between wood and aluminum. They have a greater durability than either wood or aluminum and can be bent to the breaking point without warping. The hunter who doesn't take extra-special care of his equipment should use the fiberglass shafts. He can throw them in the back of his truck, sit on them, get them wet, and still not have to worry as long as the fletching stays on and the broadhead (point) stays sharp. However, if a fiberglass arrow is not straight when it comes from the manufacturer, it stays that way because there is no way to straighten it. Another disadvantage of the fiberglass shaft is its tendency to shatter or split if it hits a hard object such as a rock.

Aluminum Arrows

Aluminum arrows are the most expensive of the three types of shafts and are used by both target archers and bowhunters. Special care has to be taken not to warp aluminum arrows, but there is a tool available that will straighten them if they do become warped. Since aluminum arrows are lighter than wood or fiberglass, some bowhunters do not feel confident that they will penetrate as deeply as the heavier wood or fiberglass shafts. This is an argument I won't get into. I do know, however, that many deer have been killed with all three types: wood, fiberglass, and aluminum.

Regardless of the type of arrow shaft the archer may choose, he must remember that it has to be straight to be effective. Before entering the deer woods, make sure that each arrow has been shot many times. Mark the consistently errant arrows so they will be shot at game only after all of the better arrows have been used. A quick way to check an arrow for straightness is to place the tips of the thumb and second finger on the left hand together and bend them inward toward the palm of the hand. This will form a V with the fingernails up. Lay the front part of the arrow in this V, hold the arrow nock with the fingers of the right hand, and give the nock a spin while pushing the shaft forward. A straight arrow will glide smoothly across the fingernails of the V while a bent shaft will cause the arrow to bounce.

Arrow Spine

The most important factor to keep in mind when purchasing an arrow is its flexibility or "spine." The spine of the arrow must match the bow weight for proper shooting and for safety reasons. When the arrow is released from the bow, it must bend a certain amount in order to absorb the pressure released by the forward movement of the bowstring, then the arrow must be flexible enough to recover or straighten out after it clears the bow.

An arrow that has too much flexibility or spine will not bend properly as it leaves the bow and will usually be off target to the left (for right-handed shooters). An arrow with too little spine will bend too much and will usually be off target to the right. Also, an underspined arrow may break and hurt the shooter or someone else.

Archery dealers have charts that will show the archer the exact spine needed for various bow weights, arrow lengths, and arrow materials. These charts are prepared by the manufacturers after many hours of testing. If at all possible, use

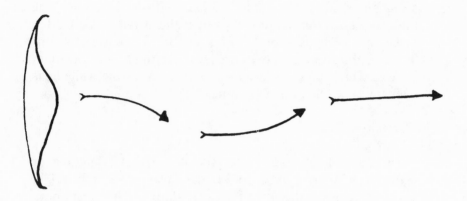

The diagram shows an arrow bending as it leaves the bow, then recovering and continuing its true flight.

the spine requirements recommended by the manufacturers, keeping in mind that it is much better to use an arrow that is overspined than to use one that is underspined.

PARTS OF AN ARROW

A bowhunter doesn't have to know the various parts of an arrow to be able to kill a deer, but among archers it is a lot easier if certain parts of the arrow are called common agreed-upon names. For example, the crest should be called the crest rather than "that strip of paint on the end of the arrow where the feathers are." The beginner should familiarize himself with the common names given to the parts of an arrow.

Nock

The nock is the plastic tip on the end of the arrow that fits onto the string to hold it in place until the arrow is released. There are several designs of nocks available, but the two most popular designs are the Bjorn nock that snaps lightly over the string and holds the arrow in place until it is released, and the open-end nock that merely slips over the string and is held in place by the fingers or by pressure from the string. For hunting, the Bjorn is most popular since the hunter does not have to worry about his arrow falling off the string while he is stalking or waiting for an animal.

Fletching

The part of an arrow after the nock is the fletching or feathers. Today's modern arrows may have lightweight plastic fletching rather than feathers, although the most popular fletching material is still turkey feathers. The fletching may be purchased in many different colors; for bowhunting, a yellow or orange fletching is easier to spot in the brush.

The fletching on an arrow serves as a rudder to keep the arrow in line as it flies from the bow to the target. On most commercial arrows there are three feathers attached to the shaft in a manner so that one feather (the cock feather) will point directly away from the bow when the arrow is nocked. The other two feathers (the hen feathers) will lay fairly parallel with the bow so they will slide past the handle without the arrow being deflected. On most arrows, the cock feather is a different color than the hen feathers, so it can be easily spotted when nocking the arrow.

Some archers prefer to use a four-feathered fletching instead of the standard three. They contend that four feathers give their arrows greater stability in flight.

Crest

As noted, the crest of an arrow is merely "that strip of paint on the end of the arrow where the feathers are." It serves no useful purpose except to beautify the arrow or to identify an arrow as belonging to a matched set or to a certain individual. Most bowhunters prefer not to have a crest at all or at least to use one of a dark color.

ARROW POINTS

Moving down the body or "shaft" of the arrow, we come to the last but certainly not the least important part of an arrow—the point. There are several types of points used on today's arrows with many variations of each type. The four most popular types are the target point (used for target archery), the field point (used for taking small game or target practice), the blunt (used for small game), and the broadhead (used for large game).

The Target Point

The target point as shown above fits flush with the arrow and is simply a tapered piece of metal that gives the arrow a sharp point. As the name implies, this point is intended for target archery and should never be used for game hunting of any type. Target points come in various shaft diameters that

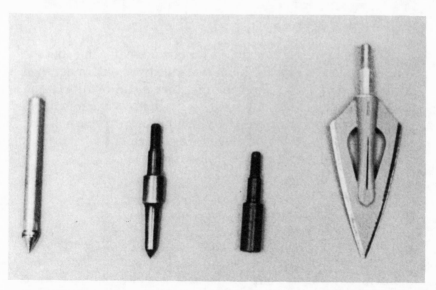

Arrow points. From left to right: target point, field point, blunt, and broadhead.

correspond to the different arrow shaft diameters, so that the point fits tightly without being forced over the arrow tip or into the shaft itself if the arrow is hollow.

The Field Point

Field points are used by both target archers and bow-hunters. They are made of a heavier metal than target points and can be matched in gram weight to broadheads, so they make very good practice points for the bowhunter. For example, if a hunter plans to use a 125-gram broadhead during deer season, he can use a 125-gram field point for practicing. Arrows will fly a little differently when the field points are replaced with broadheads, but not drastically.

Many bowhunters prefer the use of screw inserts that fit inside the arrow and allow the point to be screwed into them. This enables the archer to change from field point to broadhead or blunt in a matter of seconds, simply by removing the field point and screwing in one of the other points.

The Blunt

Some hunters use field points for taking small game, but the preferred way is to use a blunt that kills by shock rather than penetration. Blunts are made of either metal or rubber and can be bought in various sizes and weights. Some hunters make their own by using a .38 caliber pistol cartridge hull that has been shot. It will fit snugly over the end of most arrows or it can be glued into place if it is too large.

The Broadhead

There is only one area where just about all bowhunters agree when discussing broadheads—they must be sharp. But it's the type of sharpness that causes the dispute. Some bow-hunters say razor sharp is necessary while others believe that a ragged edge is best.

Defenders of the smooth edge contend that blood vessels

and arteries bleed more freely and do not seal up as quickly as they do when cut with a ragged edge. They also believe that a ragged edge tends to pinch or seal off the arteries and vessels as it cuts through the tissue of a deer, thus causing less bleeding (much the same way as with a dull broadhead).

Proponents of the ragged edge argue that their broadheads do more damage as they rip through tissue than do broadheads that slice through the tissue. Since there have been many deer killed with broadheads sharpened both ways, suffice it to say that for a broadhead to have maximum effect, it must be sharp enough to shave hair from the bowhunter's arm.

The best way to sharpen a broadhead is to screw it into a vise to keep it from twisting, then, using a small mill file, stroke each side of each cutting edge the same number of times, rotating the head in the vise as needed. Here, again, there is argument among bowhunters as to which way to stroke the head for the best results—forward toward the point or backward toward the shaft. Fred Bear, a leading bowhunter and manufacturer of archery equipment, recommends the forward stroke. The main thing, regardless of the sharpening method used, is to get the broadhead as sharp as possible with a file, then follow up with an oilstone if desired.

Each beginning archer should experiment with various ways to sharpen broadheads until he is able to find the method that works for him. Just remember to avoid leaving a very sharp point on the broadhead, because it will tend to curl if it hits a bone. Round the point off and the head will cut on through bone and tough tissue with ease.

After the heads are sharpened, they should be coated with a thin layer of oil or petroleum jelly to keep rust from corroding the edge. When in the field each head should be resharpened after each shot with a small file or one of the sharpening devices sold at archery shops.

The actual choice of which broadhead to use can be quite a problem, because there are so many of them available. There are types with two, three, four, and even six cutting edges. There are solid types and there are types that have inserts (usually razor blades) that fit into slots precut into the head by the manufacturer. I recommend that each bowhunter go to an archery shop, look at the various heads, talk to the dealer and other experienced bowhunters, then choose a few different styles and do some experimenting until he finds the head he wants to try.

Collection of various broadheads.

Some bowhunters change types of broadheads almost as often as they change pants. The best thing to do is to find a head that can be sharpened easily, stays sharp, flies well out of the bow, and penetrates deeply into a deer. When you find one, stick with it. I personally use the Bear Razorhead, but that doesn't mean that every bowhunter will like or have the same results with it that I have had.

After a broadhead has been selected and mounted on the arrow shaft, always check to be sure that it is mounted straight. Roll the arrow on a smooth level table or board with the broadhead extended over the edge. Watch for any wobble in the head as the arrow is rotated. If there is a wobble, remove the head and remount it. A broadhead that is improperly mounted will cause the arrow to fly erratically.

ACCESSORIES

Bow and arrows are all that a bowhunter really needs to kill deer. But the new archer should consider some of the accessories that will aid him in his hunting and practicing. Archery, like any other sport, has become highly commercialized since there is money to be made, so every manufacturer of archery tackle has developed items to "help" the archer. If the archer were to buy only one of every item available, he would not be able to carry it all in a pack on his back, much less be able to use it if a deer jumped out of the brush, unless he were to throw the whole pack at the deer and club it to death.

Unless the beginning archer has an unlimited supply of money, he should buy only the accessories needed to get him started shooting. Then, as he becomes more experienced, he will be able to better determine which items he really needs and which items would only clutter his accessory box and never be used.

Armguard and Finger Protectors

In my opinion, a good armguard to protect the bow arm from the slap of the string and finger protectors for the drawing hand to keep the string from cutting into the fingers during the drawing of the bow are absolute musts for all archers, be they target or hunting archers.

All archery manufacturers produce some type of armguard and they are all similar in design—a strip of leather or plastic with straps for easy attachment and removal from the bow arm. (The bow arm is the arm that holds the bow when in a shooting position.) The armguard is worn on the inside of the forearm and prevents the string from slapping the arm when the arrow is released. It does not take a beginner long to realize the importance of the armguard. A few slaps on the forearm are usually enough to convince him.

An archer's glove or a tab is necessary for protecting the three fingers used when drawing the bowstring. Both gloves and tabs are usually made from some type of soft leather that will provide protection without hindering the release. Most hunters prefer the glove, because it is worn like any other glove. Target archers prefer the tab, which fits only on the tips of the fingers and is harder to manipulate quickly under hunting conditions. They contend that they can feel the string better with the tab than with the glove. Also, the glove is usually a little stiffer than the tab and not quite as slick.

Gloves are made in both left-handed and right-handed styles and in several sizes. Tabs are also made in left-handed and right-handed styles and are extra long so each archer will be able to cut them down to his finger length. The tab should be cut to where it just covers the tips of the fingers when they are in position on the bowstring.

Quivers

Another useful item is a quiver for carrying extra arrows. There are so many different designs on the market that the archer will have no problem finding one that he likes and that will fit the type of shooting he plans to do. There are designs made for both left- and right-handed archers.

Two things must be kept in mind when purchasing a quiver: quality and safety. Avoid cheap plastic or poor quality leather and designs that leave the arrow points exposed. Exposed points are dangerous to the archer, especially if he is carrying arrows tipped with sharp hunting broadheads.

The bow quiver was designed with the hunter in mind. It either snaps or bolts on the bow itself and carries from four to eight extra arrows, depending on the style. When purchasing a bow quiver, be sure to choose a design with a strong hood that covers the arrow points. There are some designs on the market that leave the points exposed and, as mentioned before, this is dangerous. If the hunter should accidentally fall, he could receive a bad cut from the heads or cut his bowstring or even wound someone else. I have seen this happen too many times.

Here are some of the basic quiver designs that are on the market today.

When most archers hear the word "quiver," they think of the back quiver (not shown in the photo) because it is the design that more closely resembles the quivers used by Indians. There are two principal designs of back quivers: one where the arrows are removed over the shoulder of the archer, and one where the arrows are removed from the bottom of the quiver by reaching around the waist. Most of the back-quiver styles carry twelve or more extra arrows without crowding.

Side quivers are designed for target archery or for hunting. Some styles have clips that hold the arrows in place while others carry the arrows loose. Most of them are equipped with loops or clips for a belt.

The hip pocket quiver is used mainly for target archery where only target or field points are needed. It is not a practical quiver for carrying broadheads, because it fits into the hip pocket of the archer's pants and would cause him some agony if he should sit down on the sharp heads and they cut through the quiver and into his flesh.

Do not carry more arrows than the quiver was designed to carry, because the arrows will be crowded and difficult to draw one at a time. Also, broadheads may be dulled by scraping against other arrows. Many quivers are designed with accessory pockets, which is a handy place to carry small items, but do not try to carry too much in them or they will cause the quiver to become very heavy before the day is over.

String Silencers

String silencers come in various designs and are used to help muffle bowstring noise when the arrow is released by absorbing much of the string vibration. Place one silencer on each end of the bowstring near the point where the string touches the limbs.

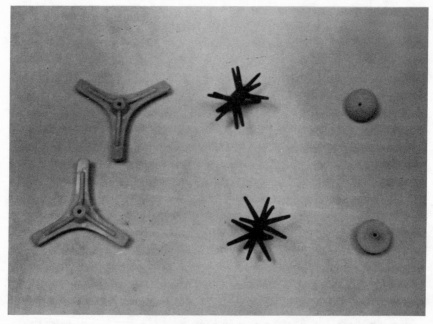

String silencers and brush buttons.

Accessories

Brush Buttons

Brush buttons are small rubber balls that slide on the bow string and fit up next to the tip of each limb. They prevent leaves and small twigs from catching between the string and the bow tips as the hunter moves through the woods.

Arrow Holder

Many bowhunters, myself included, use an arrow holder to keep the arrow in place without the use of the fingers. This allows the arrow to be ready for a quick shot without the archer having to sit for hours with his finger on the arrow to hold it on the string. As the string is drawn the arrow holder releases the arrow quickly and without noise.

Bow Cover

A bow cover helps to camouflage the bow and at the same time protect it from being scratched by limbs and briars as the hunter moves through the woods.

Other Equipment

After one or two trips to the deer woods, the bowhunter will be able to determine which items he should take with him. Below is a list of items that the serious bowhunter will carry in his accessory kit every time he goes hunting. They do not take much room and can be left in the car or at camp when the hunter is in the woods. (Items already discussed in detail are not included in the list.)

1. Bowstring wax
2. Extra feathers and nocks
3. Feather and nock cement
4. Fletching tool
5. File and whetstone for sharpening broadheads
6. Extra broadheads
7. Small pair of pliers

8. Cement for points and broadheads
9. Extra bowstring (already broken in)
10. Insect repellent and snake-bite kit (optional)
11. Five or six feet of good strong rope

Other items such as clothing, camping gear, food, flashlights, knives, and the like will depend on the type of weather the archer will be hunting in and the length of time he will be gone from home. Those items will be much the same for bowhunters as for rifle hunters.

The archer need only to visit an archery shop to see dozens of helpful aids to the bowhunter. But he should be very careful when selecting accessories and choose only good-quality items that will be used regularly.

PART II

HOW TO
SHOOT

PROFESSIONAL HELP, BOOKS, CLUBS

Archery is not an easy sport to learn without a little help. Very few people are able to buy a bow, go out into their backyard, and become a good archer, but with proper instruction, a lot of reading, and many hours of practice, a beginner can become proficient enough with a bow to go into the woods and bring back game.

The best way to learn to shoot a bow is through the instructions of a professional who makes his living, or at least a portion of it, by teaching others how to shoot. A good instructor knows his business and can get a beginner started right. This type of instruction can be expensive and can cost more than the average hunter can afford. Another, less expensive way to get professional help is through a local Y.M.C.A., many of which offer classes in archery at a very nominal fee.

If professional help cannot be obtained, then the novice should read a few of the countless books available that can teach him how to shoot. These books are advertised in outdoor magazines and can be found in bookstores and libraries. Although it is very difficult for a beginner to learn how to shoot solely with written instructions, it can be done if he is determined enough and will practice enough.

Also, in almost every town there is either a well-organized archery club or a group of archers who get together regularly to practice and discuss the art of shooting a bow. The beginner should seek out one of these clubs. Most of them are filled with nice people who not only enjoy the sport, but are always looking for new members. The novice can learn more from them in a few hours than he can teach himself in days. Many members of local archery clubs are also avid bowhunters who can teach him how to shoot as well as help him learn some of the important things that an archer must know before he can expect to bag deer: how to hunt, how deer react to various situations, when to shoot, where to aim, and how to field-dress a deer.

BRACING THE BOW

Before learning the various steps necessary to shoot properly, the beginning archer must know the correct way to brace (string) his bow. There are basically three methods used to brace a bow, and if done carefully any one of them can be used without damage to the bow or to the archer. These are the push-and-pull method, the step-across method, and the use of a bow stringer.

Bracing the bow—the push-and-pull method.

To begin the push-and-pull method, place the tip of the lower bow limb on the edge of the shoe at the instep of the right foot. (Left-handed archers should reverse this procedure.) This end of the bow should have the string in place and held with a rubber band or string keeper to prevent it from slipping before bracing begins. The back of the bow must be pointing upwards. Grasp the handle of the bow with the right hand and pull upwards while pushing downwards with the left hand on the upper bow limb. This pressure will cause the bow to bend and allow the archer to slip the string into its groove on the upper limb with the fingers of the left hand.

Although this method is used by many archers, it is the most difficult to learn and the most likely method to cause bow or personal damage. If the archer should allow the bow to slip before the string is properly set in its grooves, the limb could twist or slap backwards hitting the archer in the face or shoulder.

Bracing the bow—the step-across method.

The step-across method is safer than the push-and-pull method and doesn't require as much arm strength since the hips apply most of the pressure. Place the curve of the bow's lower limb over the top side of the left foot while holding the upper limb with the right hand. (The back of the bow must be facing the archer.) Step across—or over—the bow with the right leg so the handle of the bow will rest across the right hip and the string will be held in front of the body by the left hand. The lower string loop must be in the groove on the lower limb and held by a string keeper. Apply pressure to the bow by bending the body so the hips will push out against the handle while the right hand pushes forward on the upper limb. When the bow is bent far enough, the upper string loop can be slipped into place with the left hand.

Bracing the bow—the bow stringer.

The most practical method of bracing a bow for beginners, women, and children is with a bow stringer. Most experienced archers recommend it above all other methods. The bow stringer is simply a long cord with leather pockets on each end. With the bow handle facing upward, place the leather pockets over each tip of the bow with the string hanging down. The archer places one foot on the middle of the stringer and pulls upward on the bow handle. This will cause the bow to bend and the upper string loop that is already over the bow limb (the purpose of the larger loop on one end of the string) can be slipped easily into place. Regardless of which bracing method an archer uses, he must check to be sure that both string loops are properly seated in their grooves before he releases the pressure. Otherwise, the string may slip and cause expensive damage to the bow or painful injury to the archer. Beginners should have an experienced archer instruct them before trying to brace their bows alone.

FISTMELE

After the bow has been braced and before starting to shoot, the archer should check the fistmele, which is the distance between the bow handle and the string. In olden times the archer used his fist with the thumb extended to check this height, and that is how the term "fistmele" originated. The fistmele is important and must always be checked for the simple reason that a bow will perform more smoothly, cause less arm slap, and have less string noise when the string is of the proper length. A fistmele that is too high means that the string will be too short, or if the fistmele is too low, the string will be too long. A height of four to six inches is suitable on most bows. However, each bow is different and the archer should check the manufacturer's specifications for the exact height. Most manufacturers indicate the proper height for the fistmele on their bows.

To make the string longer or shorter in order to adjust the fistmele to its proper height, twist the string tighter or loosen it before bracing the bow. If this doesn't adjust the string length properly, a new string should be purchased.

LEARNING TO SHOOT PROPERLY

There are basically five steps that must be mastered before a person will be able to shoot properly. By "properly," I mean well enough to hit a deer in a vital spot. These five steps are: (1) stance, (2) nocking the arrow, (3) drawing the bow, (4) holding and aiming, and (5) release and follow-through. If the beginner does not develop all five steps in the correct manner, his shooting will be erratic and disappointing, which may lead to a loss of interest in archery.

Some beginners are very receptive and are able to develop their shooting form quickly, while others feel uncomfortable at first and must spend considerable time practicing before their form is perfected. Often the slow starters end up being the best archers, because they tend to concentrate more on what they are doing. As a result, they can tell when they do something wrong and they are able to correct it.

The Stance

At first, the classical stance for shooting a bow and arrow is uncomfortable for most beginning archers, but after a few practice sessions it starts to feel more natural, and the archer begins to assume the position with no problem.

For the proper stance, both feet should be spread just enough to allow good balance, with the toes of both feet pointing directly in front of the archer at a 90-degree angle to the target. The head should be held erect and turned to face the target with the left shoulder (for right-handed shooters) pointing directly at the target.

From this position the archer is able to draw the bow and look directly down the arrow at the target (see photo).

It may seem a little peculiar to discuss the importance of the way a bowhunter should stand, because under actual hunting conditions it is next to impossible for an archer to use the classical upright position, especially if he is in a tree. However, it is best for the beginner to use the correct stance while learning to shoot. Then, after he can keep his arrows in a fairly close

Classical stance.

group at 10, 15, 20, and 30 yards using the classical stance, he should practice various positions that may be needed in the deer woods.

If the bowhunter plans to hunt from a tree, he should practice from an elevated position. He will discover that shooting from a tree is entirely different from shooting on the ground. Most shots will have a tendency to go high, so the archer must aim lower. He should practice shooting at objects or targets as far away from the tree as 40 yards and as close under the tree as possible. I have had to shoot at deer that were directly beneath me, and that is one of the most difficult shots to make with a bow and arrow. Needless to say, my stance was somewhat inverted.

A bowhunter should also practice shooting from a kneeling position, a sitting position, a twisted position, and any other way that he can imagine. No amount of practice is too much, and it is almost impossible to determine ahead of time exactly where a deer will appear, so the hunter must be able to shoot from any angle if he plans to bring home meat. Of course, there is always the exception to the rule, where a deer will walk out broadside to a hunter and allow a perfect shot. But since those chances are few and far between, the hunter should be prepared to shoot from any stance short of standing on his head and his chances for success will be much higher. While learning, he should use the classical stance.

Nocking the Arrow

To some beginners nocking the arrow may seem too elementary to require elaboration. However, it is an important step and it must be done properly.

1. Hold the bow in the left hand with the string close to the body.
2. With the right hand, take an arrow by the nock and lay it on the bow shelf or arrow rest.
3. Rotate the arrow until the cock feather is up, as discussed in the previous chapter.
4. Slip the nock onto the string at the nocking point.

The arrow is now ready to be shot, and under no circumstances should it ever be pointed in the direction of another person or at anything that can be damaged by an arrow.

Drawing the Bow

After an arrow has been nocked, place the index finger of your right hand on the string above the arrow and the next two fingers below the arrow with the string laying in the finger creases between the first and second joints.

The archer is now in the "ready" position. The left hand should be holding the bow while the left index finger keeps the

Archer in the ready position.

arrow in place on the arrow shelf or rest. The fingers of the right hand should be in place on the string.

To complete the draw, raise and extend the left arm to shoulder height at the same time locking the elbow joint.

With the right arm (shoulder and back muscles doing most of the work) draw the bowstring straight back to the anchor point, keeping the hand and forearm straight and the elbow at shoulder height.

The anchor point is some spot on the face that serves as an indicator for a completed draw. Bowhunters usually touch the corner of their mouth with the index finger of the drawing hand. Other archers use various spots that feel comfortable. Regardless of where the anchor point is, the archer must draw to that point each time he shoots, in order to be consistent.

Archer in the raised position (above) and at the full draw with corner-of-the-mouth anchor (below).

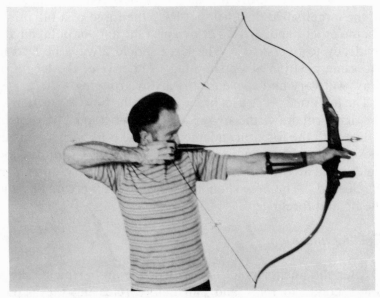

The full draw high-cheek anchor (above), and under-cheek anchor (below).

Arrows released before the anchor point is reached fall short of the target since they will not have the force of a full draw. On the other hand, arrows drawn past the anchor point have a tendency to overshoot. The head should always be held in the same position when shooting. Otherwise, the length of draw will vary and cause erratic arrow grouping.

The left arm serves as a brace to hold the bow in position as the right arm draws the arrow. The left wrist must be straight in line with the forearm and must hold the bow with a firm but loose grip as the bow is drawn. If the bow is gripped too rigidly, the arrow will be thrown to one side or the other as it is released. The bow should rest on the web created by the thumb and forefinger.

Holding and Aiming

After the anchor point is reached, the archer must take a few seconds to relax and aim before releasing the arrow. This pause is known as the "hold" and is very important for consistent shooting. Regardless of the type of aiming the archer uses, it takes a few seconds of hold to get on target.

As a rule, target archers using light bows and sights and shooting at stationary targets take a longer hold than do bow-hunters who must be able to aim faster since they will be shooting at moving targets. However, the bowhunter must also hold momentarily in order to aim properly.

Many beginning archers have a tendency to release the arrow as soon as their anchor point is reached, or before, with no hold at all. This is referred to as "snap-shooting" and is a very bad habit to get into, as well as a hard one to break.

Snap-shooting can also be caused by an archer being over-bowed (trying to shoot a bow that is too heavy for him). If the snap-shooting malady cannot be overcome by practice, a lighter bow should be used until the muscles required for shooting are built up; then a heavier bow can be tried again. If snap-shooting is still present after changing to a lighter bow, the problem is a habit and can be overcome only by the archer himself. He must concentrate on holding for a few seconds each time a shot is taken, until he is able to hold without thinking about it.

There are three major methods used for aiming: instinctive, gap, and with bowsights, either hunting sights or target sights. Since it is not practical to use target sights for hunting, they will not be discussed.

Instinctive Aiming

Most deer hunters use either the instinctive or gap method. Instinctive aiming is impossible to teach, because there is no real way of explaining how it is done. The archer just feels where the arrow should go and is able to elevate his bow to the correct height to put the arrow into the target. This sounds very confusing, I know, but it is true. I am an instinctive shooter myself and only after many hours of practice at targets from 5 feet to 40 yards away was I able to hit with a fair degree of accuracy.

Instinctive archers, in most cases, are not as adept at putting arrow after arrow into a very small target as are other types of shooters, but they are usually very good at bringing home meat. They do not have to know the exact distance to their target, they just know from practice where the arrow will go, which is a very good method to use in the woods.

Gap Aiming

To use the gap method, the archer must be able to judge distance fairly well. After determining the distance, he aims either above, below, or directly at the target by using the tip of his arrow as a sight. Like instinctive shooters, the gap shooter must practice a great deal and be able to concentrate on the spot where he wants his arrow to hit.

Bowsights

There are many very good bowsights on the market for the bowhunter to choose from if he decides that he wants to use a sight rather than the instinctive or gap method of aiming. The basic design for most bowsights is a bar that attaches to the bow handle with one or more sight pins that can be adjusted up or down the bar for different distances (usually from 20 to 40 yards). The pins can also be moved in or out to adjust for arrows grouping to the left or right of the target.

An adjustable bowsight.

To set the bowsights, measure off a distance of 20 yards from the target, set the first or top pin on the bar to about where it should be. (This will have to be a guess.) After the pin is set, nock an arrow, aim at the target (trying to hold the tip of the pin on the center of the target), and shoot. Hopefully, the arrow will strike somewhere on the target.

As an example, let's say that the arrow hit low and to the right of center on the target. To adjust the sight pin after the first arrow, move it up on the bar and screw it out. In other words, move the pin in the direction the arrow should go to hit the target center.

After the adjustment has been made, shoot a second arrow. Let's say that the second arrow hit a little high and a little to the left of center. To adjust the sight pin after the second shot, move it down and screw it in.

If all other points of the archer's form are good, the next arrow should hit fairly close to the center of the target. From this point on, do not adjust the sight after every shot, because there could be some reason other than the sight that causes the arrow to miss. Shoot several groups of five arrows before deciding if the sight pin should be moved again.

To set the bowsight's remaining pins, measure off the desired distance and follow the same procedure as setting for the

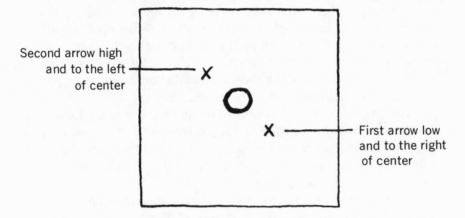

Adjusting the bowsight.

20-yard distance. It is not practical to set sight pins for distances of more than 40 yards, because most shots taken by bowhunters at deer are 40 yards or less—usually much less!

The bowhunter who uses a hunting sight must be able to judge distances very well. Otherwise, his shots will be off. For example, if a deer is standing 30 yards from the hunter and the 20-yard pin is used, the arrow will fall short by several feet. By practice, the hunter will be able to learn how to estimate distances and also learn where to hold the sight pins for distances that fall between the set ranges.

Of the three methods for aiming that have been discussed, the instinctive method is by far the most practical to use in the deer woods, but not many archers are able to develop the feel needed to aim instinctively, so each person should choose his own method and learn it well through lots of practice.

Release and Follow-Through

After the archer has drawn the bow until his finger touches the anchor point, has held for a few seconds, and has properly aimed, he is ready to release the arrow. To release the arrow, he simply relaxes the three fingers holding the string and lets it slip off the finger tips smoothly. He should avoid jerking the string or moving the hand away from the face. If the release is done right, there should be no body movement at all except the backward motion of the hand as the tension is removed. In the correct follow-through the archer does not move at all until the arrow strikes the target. The bow should stay at the full draw position and the drawing hand should remain where it stops its backward motion after the release.

Too many beginners as well as experienced archers tend to drop the bow arm as soon as they release the arrow, so they can watch the arrow hit the target. This is a bad habit to get into and like snap-shooting it is very difficult to remedy except through concentration and practice.

A poor release and follow-through can cause an archer much frustration, because it is one of the hardest steps in shooting to detect and correct. The best way to detect this problem is to have a buddy watch the archer as he shoots several arrows, then tell him what he is doing wrong.

Practice Methods

After learning the five basic steps for shooting a bow, the archer can only become a proficient shooter after many hard hours of practice. Any seasoned bowhunter will attest that there is no such thing as too much practice. Regardless of how much a hunter practices, he will never be perfect, and too little practice can and will cost him many fine trophies that otherwise could have been easy targets. A bowhunter should practice the year around. Of course, die-hard hunting archers do not really get any excitement out of target practice.

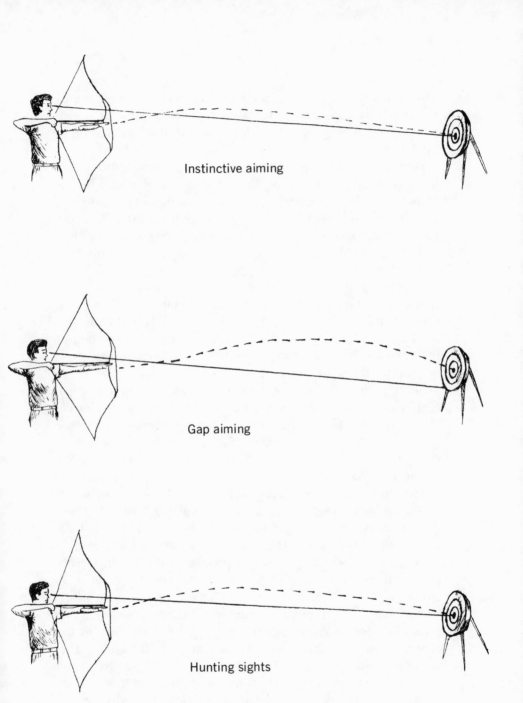

Instinctive aiming

Gap aiming

Hunting sights

Three methods of aiming.

They think it is a waste of their time to punch holes in paper. But there are countless other ways to prepare for deer season without becoming bored with stationary targets set up at known distances.

One of the best ways to practice for big-game hunting is to hunt for small game during the off season. Rabbits, for example, are a big challenge. They are fast-moving, hard-to-hit targets and will quickly show the archer how much he needs to practice. If a hunter can consistently bring down bunnies at 15 to 20 yards, then he should have little trouble hitting a deer at the same distance.

Another good way to practice is to bowfish. Gar, carp, frogs, snakes, and turtles make very fine targets. The tackle used for taking this type of game is much different from that used for deer, but the habit of careful aiming is developed on these small fish and reptiles and is easily transferred over when deer tackle is used.

Some archers get a great deal of satisfaction from participating in award programs offered by some of the national archery clubs that allow the hunter to win patches, pins, and medals for the game he takes. One of the best programs is the Art Young Award Program offered to members of the National Field Archery Association (NFAA). This program allows an archer to work his way up to a Master Bowhunter by taking various small and large game with a bow. Later in this guide is an excerpt from the NFAA rule book that describes the Art Young Program. Join it, you'll like it.

There are also many ways to practice with inanimate objects without becoming bored. One challenging target is an old tire rigged with a cardboard center and rolled down a long sloping hill. The tire will bounce, wobble, and turn much like a running deer. An archer is pretty good if he can hit the center of the tire three out of five times at 20 yards. This method of practice requires two people since one has to roll the tire down the hill. The archer doing the shooting should be sure that he does not release an arrow until his partner is safely out of the way.

If the hunter lives in the city and cannot hunt for small game or has no place to roll tires down a hill, he may have to be content with punching holes in a paper target. Even so, he doesn't have to use regular targets. There are life-sized animal targets available for both small- and large-game animals, or the archer can draw his own target on a large piece of cardboard. Animal targets are excellent for practice, because they allow the archer to concentrate on vital areas of the game when he is aiming. (See the section of this book on arrow placement for a discussion of the vital areas of deer.)

A bowhunter must never get into the habit of shooting from known distances. He should practice enough to be able to tell exactly where his arrow will hit a target from any distance up to about 40 yards without knowing the exact number of yards. Shots at deer over 40 yards are chance shots and are not recommended under most conditions. Of course, an archer using a bowsight must be able to determine the approximate distance or he will not be able to determine which sight bar to use.

It is also very important for a bowhunter to practice at various angles to the target. Broadside shots at a deer are few and far between, so the archer should be able to adjust for left- and right-angle shots as well as for shots from above if he plans to use a tree stand. The archer, to shoot well from a tree, must learn to aim lower than he would if he were standing on the ground. Otherwise, he will find that the arrow will go too high and his deer will speed away untouched.

If no trees are available for practicing, the archer needs only to use his imagination to find something high enough to shoot from. The top of a truck, the house, or even a well-anchored ladder will get him off the ground high enough for practicing.

Regardless of what type of practicing the hunter chooses to do, it is very important for him to remember to do it safely and to do a lot of it. Also, he should practice in his hunting clothes. No serious bowhunter will go into the deer woods not knowing what his bow will do and not having practiced in the clothes that he will be wearing. It may seem a bit ridiculous to wear full camouflage hunting clothes for practice in the middle of July, but it is much more ridiculous to shoot at a nice buck and miss because the string hits a loose sleeve or catches on a button that the archer has not noticed.

Commercial (above) and homemade (below) deer targets.

Shooting Errors

One of the main reasons archers miss the target consistently is because they fail to learn from their misses and do not try to find out why they are missing. If an archer's arrows group high time after time, then there is a reason for it. He is doing something wrong, and with a little thinking he can correct the problem and bring his group down. The same holds true for a group to the left, right, low, or no group at all.

The problem may exist either in his equipment or in his form, or both. The following checklist will help the archer to find and solve many of his problems. It may take long hours of practice, because each point on the checklist will have to be tried until the arrows begin to group in the correct place. The archer may also discover that there are several reasons that are causing his arrows to group wrong. He should not become discouraged, but should work them out one by one.

All of the following faults apply to right-handed shooters. Left-handed archers should reverse the left and right strike patterns.

Grouping pattern.

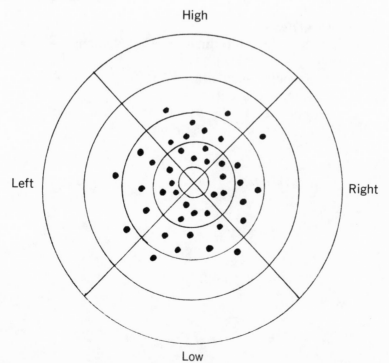

I. ARROWS GROUPING TO THE LEFT
Equipment Problems
1. Arrows overspined
2. Fletching too short
3. Arrow rest too far back
4. Sight pin too far in

Form Problems
1. Bowstring interference, strikes clothing or armguard
2. Loss of tension in back muscles
3. Gripping bow too tight
4. Wrist turned in too far
5. Plucking string
6. Moving anchor point to the right
7. Bow canted to left
8. Moving bow hand to the left on release

II. ARROWS GROUPING TO RIGHT
Equipment Problems
1. Arrows underspined
2. Arrow rest too far forward
3. Fistmele too low
4. Sight pin too far out

Form Problems
1. Shooting glove too thick, causing plucking
2. Peeking
3. Anchor point moved left
4. Bow canted to right
5. Bow hand too far to the left on the bow handle
6. Moving bow hand to the right on release

III. ARROWS GROUPING HIGH
Equipment Problems
1. Nocking point too low
2. Sight pin too low

Form Problems
1. Overdrawing
2. Lowering anchor point

3. Raising bow arm at release
4. Heeling
5. Downward release
6. Head too far back causing overdraw

IV. ARROWS GROUPING LOW
Equipment Problems
1. Nocking point too high
2. Bow weight too heavy for full draw
3. Sight pin too high

Form Problems
1. Underdrawing
2. Allowing arrow to creep forward before release
3. Dropping bow arm as soon as arrow is released
4. Head too far forward, causing underdraw

V. NO ARROW GROUPING AT ALL
Equipment Problems
1. Nocking point loose
2. Sight pin loose

Form Problems
1. Not aiming
2. Not holding before release
3. Not anchoring at the same place on each shot
4. Moving head
5. Opening or closing mouth, causing anchor point to change
6. Flinching at time of release

These are only a few of the reasons why an arrow does not strike the target every time, and as can be seen from the list, there are more form faults than equipment faults, assuming that the bow and the arrows are of good quality to begin with. If an archer is having a problem, he should not give up but should just work it out and keep practicing. Another archer can watch him as he shoots. Often they will be able to spot a fault that he doesn't realize exists.

One thing that must be remembered when trying to correct shooting errors is the wind. It may not be the archer's equipment or his form that is causing him to miss, but the wind blowing his arrows off target. But he shouldn't use this as an excuse for bad shooting.

PART III

THE
WHITETAIL
DEER

Up to this point, we have been concerned only with the equipment and shooting style needed for bowhunting. Indeed, proper equipment and form are important to successful bowhunting. But even if an archer has learned all of the preceding sections so well that he can repeat them almost word for word, and has learned to shoot so well that he can place five out of five arrows inside a three-inch circle at 20 yards, he still will not kill a deer if the deer can't be found.

To be a successful bowhunter, an archer must learn how to find deer, which is not an easy task, and a person can certainly believe the hunter who says that the whitetail deer is one of the most difficult of North American large-game animals to find if it does not want to be found. From the moment a deer is born, there is a constant threat to its life, so it has a right to make itself hard to find.

Nature provides many pitfalls for the deer. Not only do they have to scrounge for food during several months of each year and try to keep from freezing to death when the cold winter months arrive, they also have to be on constant alert for predators. Wolves, wild dogs, bobcats, cougars, and other predatory animals love to feed on deer, especially young fawns, and they account for many deer deaths each year.

Aside from natural threats to the safety of the deer, there is man. Man is a threat to the whitetail, not just by hunting, which accounts for only a fraction of the deer killed by men each year, but by indirect threats. Highways, fences, and pollution are the major causes of deer deaths presented by man and his constant encroachment of deer territory.

As a result of these, plus countless other potential threats to their lives, whitetail deer have developed a very sensitive system of nerves, senses, and instincts that has enabled them to survive even within the limits of great metropolitan areas. For a hunter to be able to outwit one of these wily creatures, he must know something of the nature, habits, and physical makeup of the animal. Otherwise, he may wander around in woods filled with deer and never see anything except their tracks.

DISTRIBUTION

Although the habits of the whitetail may vary somewhat in different areas of the country, they are basically the same whether the deer resides in New York, Florida, Oregon, or Texas.   The whitetail's range covers the entire land area shown on the map except the shaded portions.

The whitetail's range extends over the entire non-shaded portion of the map.

BREEDING HABITS

In the fall of the year as the days begin to turn cool and crisp, the whitetail bucks start to become restless. They start roaming the woods more, their necks begin to swell, they start shadow-boxing with small trees and low-hanging limbs, and every other buck becomes an enemy. The rutting season is on and they are ready for romance.

The rutting season is the period when deer mate. It comes once a year and lasts about one month. The exact time may vary from one part of the country to another. For example, it may come as much as a month earlier in northern states than in southern states.

The rutting season is the only time a buck is really in a fighting mood as well as a romantic one. The remainder of the year he spends eating, sleeping, and staying out of danger. However, during the rut, each buck establishes a certain area where he considers himself master, and he will fight any other buck that challenges his right to that area and to the does within its boundaries.

By the time the rut gets into full swing, the antlers of the buck have hardened and lost their velvet. (See the section on antlers for a discussion of antler development.) In his restless mood, the buck wants to fight, so he uses his antlers as a weapon and many small trees and bushes fall victim to his moods. The buck will scrape, twist, and rub his antlers on a small tree as if it were another buck and he is trying to over-power it. This method of play-fighting helps to strengthen the muscles in the buck's neck and sharpen his antlers for the real battles that he will face in the future while he is protecting his territory.

As the rut progresses, the buck's neck will continue to swell as more and more blood collects there. Also, the testicles will drop in preparation for the rutting animal's forthcoming acts of reproduction.

A rutting buck will paw out a place on the ground approximately one to four feet in diameter. These cleared places are known as "deer scrapes" and are usually found underneath low hanging limbs or in thickets. The scrapes are void of any grass, leaves, or twigs. After the buck has cleared his scrape, he will urinate in it, making sure that the urine runs down over the musk and metatarsal glands on his legs. If the buck is very excited, he will wallow in the scrape, mixing the urine and gland secretions into the dirt. He may even ejaculate and mix that with the other ingredients.

Usually, a mature buck will make several scrapes throughout his territory. They serve a dual purpose: to let other bucks know that he is master of that area, and to attract does. He will visit each of the scrapes daily or at least every other day, hoping to find that a doe has been there or is waiting for him to return.

If instead of a doe, the buck finds another male deer near his scrape, a battle will follow to determine which of the two bucks will be master of the area. The battles are seldom fought to the death and tend to be more like shoving contests to see which buck is more powerful and can drive the other away. However, the antlers are capable of inflicting wounds that may cause the death of an unfortunate fighter if he is gored.

Often the antlers of the two battling bucks will become locked together in such a way that they will not separate. When this happens both bucks will die an agonizing death by starvation. A hunter should never try to dislodge the tangled antlers of two bucks because he may be attacked and seriously injured by one or both bucks when they are freed.

When a buck returns to a scrape and finds a visiting doe, he usually becomes very excited and may even hop around on stiff legs, snort, and wallow in the scrape again. He will then follow the doe, and the mating begins. The mating will continue until the doe goes out of heat at which time the buck will leave her to return to his scrapes and to another doe. This pattern will continue until all of the does in the buck's territory are pregnant or no longer in heat.

The role of the doe during the rutting season is very simple and less dramatic than that of the buck even though she must bear the offspring later. When she comes in heat, she will find a buck scrape and urinate in it. She then either waits for the buck to return or moves on slowly to another scrape, knowing that the buck will follow her as soon as he discovers that she has been to the scrape.

The gestation period for the whitetail deer is approximately 200 days, which means that the fawns are born in the spring. A young doe may have only one fawn, but as she grows older, she will usually give birth to two at a time. It is not uncommon for a doe to have triplets.

As soon as the fawns are born, the doe licks them dry with her tongue and allows them to nurse. Within a few minutes, the fawns are able to walk even though they are still very wobbly.

The newborn fawn is completely dependent upon its mother for food and protection, and the first 10 to 15 days of its life are spent in hiding. Due to its natural camouflage and spotted coat, it is easy for the fawn to remain unseen by most predators, especially man, so its mother simply finds a good hiding place and leaves it while she continues her daily routines. Of course, she does not stray very far from her fawn and returns frequently to be sure that it is safe and to let it nurse.

If a person is lucky enough to find a newborn fawn in its hiding place, he shouldn't expect to catch it. Although the fawn is still wobbly on its long pipestem legs, it can move at a remarkable speed when it is approached.

After a couple of weeks, the fawns are strong enough to start traveling with their mother and learning the ways of the woods. Many times the doe will have to rush to the aid of her young to keep them out of trouble and out of harm's way. As the fawns travel with their mother their senses of smell, sight, and hearing are developed to determine danger of the smallest kind, and any detection of danger will send the fawn scurrying away at top speed to the protection of the doe. New fawns are very curious and eager to learn, so nothing escapes their investigation.

One of the most pleasurable sights for a woodsman is to watch a fawn investigate something that is new to it. Until the fawn has labeled the object under surveillance as being good or bad, it will continue to be curious even if the object is a man.

The Whitetail Deer

Some friends and I were doing a little preseason scouting one year when I spotted a doe feeding about 50 yards in front of us. The wind was blowing toward us and her head was down feeding, so she was not aware of our presence. We were enjoying watching the doe browse when we received an unexpected treat. Out from behind a cedar bush bounced two young fawns. They had seen us but had no idea what we were. We were probably the first humans they had ever seen, so they had to find out just what we were doing there.

The wind was blowing from their direction toward us, so they could not smell us, and since we were not making any noise as we stood there, they could not hear us. But they could see us and wasted no time in investigating.

They ran up to about 10 yards from us and stopped. They would bob their tiny heads up and down, flick their ears, sniff the air, then retreat a few yards into the cedars only to return a few minutes later to repeat the same movements. They were trying to get some kind of reaction from us so they could determine if we were a threat to them or just other woods creatures that offered them no harm. All the time the fawns were watching us, they were "talking" to each other with low gruntlike noises. (See the section on deer communication for a discussion of deer talk.)

Finally my friend could suppress a cough no longer and the fawns vanished within seconds along with their mother. The next time those fawns were confronted with a human, they would not be as curious and would consider the intruder a danger.

Shortly after young fawns begin to follow along with their mother, they begin to nibble on tender leaves and grasses from which they draw additional strength and nourishment. The doe will continue to nurse her offspring until early fall, at which time the fawns are weaned and are expected to fend for themselves. Although they may remain with her for a much longer time, they will be treated as adults and must protect themselves as well as feed themselves.

By early fall, the fawn's spotted coat will be replaced by a protective winter coat, and the spotted coat will never return.

Even though the fawn is still less than a year old, it is capable of reproduction, and often a young doe will have a fawn the following spring when she is only one year old. The young bucks do not usually breed the first year, since they are much too small to compete with the older bucks for the does.

Young bucks sometimes develop small nubbed antlers known as "buttons." Most often, antlers do not develop at all until the buck's second summer, at which time he will have spikes (one straight horn on each side of the head). Spikes on a buck's head make him legal game for hunters in most states.

SENSES AND INSTINCTS

The deer's excellent senses and instincts have enabled it to survive in the same world with the ever expanding domain of man. It may not seem possible, but there are actually more deer today than there were a hundred years ago. This is due partially to their ability to adapt to the environmental changes that have taken place as man pushed farther and farther into the wilderness. Also, the deer have grown accustomed to man and have learned how to avoid him as much as possible.

From birth the whitetail must depend on its abilities to see, hear, smell, and sense danger in order to survive. These abilities have been developed through generation after generation until today's deer is one big nerve, ready to explode at the least hint of danger.

Sense of Smell

The greatest protection a deer possesses is its nose. A deer lives in the woods from the time it is born until it dies, so it is familiar with the smell of every animal and plant that lives there. Any smell that is foreign and does not belong will send a deer bounding away without delay.

Deer, like most animals, feed with the nose pointing into the wind. Some old-time hunters say this habit lets them smell what is before them. Other hunters contend that animals feed into the wind so that the hair on their body is not ruffled by wind blowing from their backside forward. Regardless of the reason, deer usually do feed into the wind and any odor carried to them is quickly analyzed and labeled good or bad.

Not only do deer have the ability to identify each odor, their nose is so sensitive that it can pick up the slightest trace of any odor. This is a fact that hunters must constantly keep in mind, because man's odor is foreign to deer and will spook it before the hunter has a chance to get within shooting distance of his game.

Sense of Hearing

The next important sense that a deer possesses is its ability to hear. A deer is constantly flicking its ears backward and forward in order to pick up as many sounds as possible. Not only can it distinguish each smell in the woods, it can also tell if each sound it hears is natural and if it was made by a friend or a foe. For example, a singing bird is a natural sound in the woods, but a man's cough is not, and it will certainly put a deer to running. A falling tree branch will not usually bother a deer, but the scraping of a boot on a rock will alarm it.

A friend of mine once told me that he was sitting in an oak tree one morning and there were several deer feeding on the acorns below him. He noticed that falling acorns did not alarm the deer at all. Even when he dropped them on the backs of the deer, they just kept on feeding. It is natural for acorns to fall from the oak trees and the sound of them hitting the ground means nothing to a deer, except that more food is available.

However, when my friend snapped his fingers, there were no deer around within seconds. The snapping of his fingers was not a natural woods sound, and the alert ears of the deer detected it immediately.

The distance that deer can hear has been a subject of discussion by "deer experts" for years and will probably never be solved to the satisfaction of all, but it is a known fact that a careless hunter will never see a deer until it has heard him and

A buck tests the air for smell of danger.

is in a dead run in another direction, or so well hidden that it will never be detected.

Many bowhunters have said that a deer can actually hear an arrow being drawn across the arrow rest of a bow. Believe me when I say that this is true! I have had deer feeding under my tree that would spook and run without even looking up as I drew my bow, so they had to have heard the arrow sliding over the arrow rest.

Sense of Sight

Although the deer depends mainly on its ears and nose to warn it of danger, it also has very keen eyesight that should not be underestimated by the hunter. Deer are color blind, but they are able to detect the slightest movement. A well-camouflaged hunter sitting where his outline cannot be seen may have deer standing a few feet from him without seeing him, but if he moves too quickly he will be seen.

The color white is unnatural in most woodlands and even though a deer is color blind, it can detect white. A hunter should avoid wearing white or any light color. Dark clothing or camouflage hunting suits are best for bowhunting.

Whitetail deer spend their entire life within about one square mile of where they were born, so they know their home range and just about everything in it. If the deer should see something that looks strange or was not there the last time they traveled a particular route, they will become alarmed and shy away. If they see the outline of a human form, they will be gone in a flash. (See the section on tree stands and blinds for a discussion on how to prevent a deer from seeing the outline of your body.)

I had a doe walk up to within five yards of me one afternoon while I was bowhunting. I was sitting motionless on my knees behind a clump of cedar brush and the wind was blowing in my favor, so she could not hear or smell me, yet she detected my presence and knew that I was not there the last time she came that way. My outline was not very visible, so she did not know if I was alive or a stump. She stood for several seconds looking directly at me without moving a muscle trying to make up her mind whether to walk on by or go back the way she had come. When I blinked my eyes, she saw it. That small movement convinced her that I was alive, and she did not waste any time getting away from me. Since that time, I never underestimate a whitetail's ability to see.

Feel for Danger

There have been countless times when a whitetail has shied away from my stand for no apparent reason, and I am sure that every hunter can remember many times that it has happened to him. It is my opinion that a deer can just sense

This buck has just seen the hunter, who had better shoot fast.

danger without having to actually see, hear, or smell it. Of course, I have no scientific data or "expert" opinions available, but many of the experienced hunters that I have talked with over the years feel the same way I do. Others say that the deer may have gotten a faint smell of me since odors drift on the wind in all directions. Or maybe the deer heard me scrape my foot, or one of many other things that I could have done to let it know that I was there. However, when the wind is in my favor, with me sitting absolutely still, and the deer still shies away without even looking in my direction, I can only believe that it just felt my being there.

In addition to understanding the highly developed senses of the whitetail, the bowhunter should also know something about its physical characteristics and habits, such as antlers, teeth, hair, feeding and bedding habits.

PHYSICAL CHARACTERISTICS

Antlers

Many old-timers swear that the age of a buck determines the size of his rack. This is another "expert" opinion that is not true. The size of the rack and the number of points it contains depend on many things, but not the age of the deer. Mineral content of the soil, diet, and the health of the deer are the most important factors that determine the antler growth.

A buck born early in the spring will have small nubbin horns the following fall and may even have six or eight points by the second fall when it is only 18 months old. On the other hand, many old bucks will only have spikes.

The angle and diameter of the main beams usually differ somewhat between younger and older bucks. The antlers of a young buck will not be as heavy as those found on an older buck. Also, they will angle higher above the head with less forward curve. As the buck grows older, the antlers tend to be thicker and at a lower angle to the head with a wider curve.

The main purpose of antlers is to provide the buck with a weapon for fighting off rival bucks during the rutting season. After the rut is over, the buck will lose his desire for fighting and romance and his antlers will drop off. Most bucks have lost their antlers by January and at a distance cannot be distinguished from a doe. A new set of antlers is grown each year.

New antlers begin their growth in April or May and are fully developed by September, in most localities. While the antlers are growing, they are soft and full of blood, so they are easily damaged even though they are covered by a protective skin commonly referred to as "velvet." When the antlers are mature, the buck scrapes the velvet off with his hind legs, leaving the hard bony antlers. He will then begin to sharpen them by rubbing against small shrubs and saplings, known to hunters as "buck rubs." These rubs are usually found on small bushes that will spring back as the buck fights them, thus more closely simulating the advances of another buck than would a larger, more rigid tree. The new set of antlers is ready for use by the time mating season begins.

Cases are reported each year of hunters who have killed does with antlers. Antlers on a doe are rare, but when it does happen they are usually deformed due to damage received when they are in the soft stages of development. This damage is believed to be caused by the doe not being accustomed to having antlers, and as a result she will not be prepared to take care of them during their growth.

The antlers of a whitetail deer grow out of the head, sweep slightly backward, then curve forward. They have one main beam on each side that has additional points or tines that grow upward from the main beam. There is also a single tine on each beam near the base of each antler known as the brow tine or point.

The antlers of the whitetail differ from those of its cousins, the mule deer and the blacktail deer, which have a main beam on each side of the head that forks into two beams, with each of the two beams forking again. There is also a brow point on each side of their antlers.

Teeth

Although antler growth is not an indication of age, the teeth are. The following excerpt from *The Mammals of Texas* written by William B. Davis, Professor and former head of the Department of Wildlife Science at Texas A & M University, explains the development of teeth in the whitetail deer.

"One can estimate the age of whitetails up to approximately two years by examination of the teeth. At nine months of age, the fawn will be acquiring the middle pair of permanent incisors, while the remainder of the incisors as well as the premolars will be milk teeth. At this age, on either side of each jaw one molar is well developed while the second is barely breaking through the gum. At the age of 1½ years, all milk incisors have been replaced by permanent teeth. At least two molars are fully developed, while the third may be in any condition from barely emerging from the mandible to fully emerged. At the age of two years, the full set of permanent teeth is acquired. Beyond two years, age determination is somewhat uncertain. Wear of the teeth is gradual until at five years the ridges of the enamel are no longer sharp, but rise slightly and gradually above the dentine. At still later ages, the crowns of the premolars and molars rise only a short distance above the gums and the grinding surfaces are worn practically smooth."

By using the above indicators, a hunter can estimate fairly closely the age of his deer. However, with deer older than two years, it is hard to determine exact age.

A deer in the natural surroundings of the woods seldom lives to be old. They are either killed by man or by other animals, but deer in captivity have been known to live as long as 15 years. The average life span of a whitetail is somewhere around eight years.

Teeth of a young deer.

Teeth of an old deer.

Physical Characteristics

Hair

The whitetail deer sheds its hair twice a year. Its winter coat is grayish-brown in color and has long hollow hairs that offer insulating protection against the cold weather. As spring approaches, the winter coat is shed and replaced by cooler hair that is solid and thinner than the winter coat. The new hair is reddish-brown in color.

Although the color of the main coat of hair changes, there are other distinct markings that remain the same throughout the year. The face of a whitetail is usually brown with white circles around each eye and a white band behind a black nose. The bottom part of the lower lip (chin) is white, and there is a patch of white on the throat. The inside of the legs and the stomach are white, while the outside of the legs and the top part of the tail are the color of the main coat. The tail has a black stripe down the middle. The underside of the tail and the rump are white also. The main coat is darker along the back, then becomes lighter in color along the sides down toward the stomach.

With this color combination, the whitetail has a natural suit of camouflage. They are able to blend in with their surroundings, and only a trained eye can detect them when they are standing or lying still.

Size

One of the most common questions asked by beginning whitetail deer hunters is "How large are they?" This is a question that can get all kinds of replies and arguments.

The size of a whitetail deer is one thing that just about every hunter will overestimate. So many times a hunter will say, "I sure saw a big ole buck today. He stood this high." The hunter will be measuring the deer that he saw with an outstretched arm that usually shows the deer to be anywhere from chest high to shoulder high on him. That would be one large deer!

The height of an average whitetail deer at the shoulders is somewhere around 40 inches, and the average weight is approximately 140 to 150 pounds. This will vary considerably from one locality to another. Many full-grown Texas bucks do not reach a weight of 100 pounds, while a full-grown buck of the same age from a New England state may weigh as much as 300 pounds.

There are many factors that contribute to this weight difference among whitetails. The most important are deer population in a certain area, food availability, and the type of food. Farmland areas that offer a variety of greens and grains usually produce large well-fed deer.

For example, Llanno County Texas is known as the whitetail deer capital of the world. There are literally thousands of deer there, but they are small due to overpopulation and the scarcity of food. A few hundred miles northeast of Llanno County, in southwest Arkansas where there are fewer deer and more food, the deer are larger.

If you are planning to bag a trophy deer, you should limit your hunting to the less populated areas, where the deer are well fed and grow large. Your chances of getting a deer are much less, but when you do get one, it is usually in the bragging size.

Many hunters fail to see deer, because they are actually looking too high when they move through the woods or sit on their stands. Look close to the ground. That is where the deer are. Measure off 30 to 40 inches and compare it to your own height and you will have an idea of how high to look for your deer.

Speed

Most of the time a whitetail slips through the woods constantly watching, smelling, and looking for danger, and if it doesn't detect anything out of the ordinary it will slip away rather than run. However, when a deer does shift into high gear, it is difficult for most pursuers to catch.

A whitetail's top speed is between 30 and 40 miles per hour, which doesn't seem very fast unless each leaping bound is taking the deer farther and farther away from the hunter. For such a hunter, a running deer is a very discouraging sight; but for a woodsman, there is nothing more beautiful or graceful.

The whitetail is capable of taking bounds from 15 to 20 feet in length and as high as eight to ten feet. They have been known to jump straight up as high as eight feet, change directions while in the air, and come down running away at top speed.

Whitetails are also capable of running at top speed with their belly almost touching the ground. Hitting a target like that with a rifle is quite a feat, and most good bowhunters will not even attempt it. Getting a killing shot with a bow at such times has been done, but luck more than shooting ability played a big role—even if the archer will not admit it.

Many bowhunters have stated that they have seen a standing deer actually "jump their string." This is a phrase used by bowhunters that means the deer was able to move out of the way of the arrow after it was released from the bow. Even the best bows will make a "twanging" noise when the arrow is released. When a deer hears that noise, it will spook and jump and even a well-aimed arrow may miss the deer. There's no telling just how many bad misses are blamed on the deer's ability to jump the string.

Communication

Deer do talk! Although their language may not be as well developed as the human language, it does serve its purpose and with a little study a person can understand deer talk. Often a knowledge of deer language can help a hunter to determine his next move, by being able to tell what the deer is planning to do.

Most deer language is through body action rather than vocal sound. A nervous deer that has seen, heard, or smelled something that upsets it may stomp the ground. Other deer nearby will hear or see this action and also become alerted. At this point the hunter must remain motionless, because the least movement will be detected by the deer and they will bolt away.

The white "flag" is the most common part of a deer's anatomy seen by hunters. When a whitetail is ready to run from danger, it throws its tail straight up, revealing the white rump and underside of the tail. If a hunter is going to shoot, he had better do it in a hurry or he will not have a target to shoot at within a few seconds.

The raised tail of a fleeing deer will send any other deer within the area into full flight also. Often if a deer feels that it has not been seen, it will slip away without raising its tail. But when it thinks that it has been seen, up goes the tail and away goes the deer.

Other signals are also given by the deer's tail. A half-raised tail means that the deer is nervous and the hunter should be very careful to prevent being detected by the alert deer. When the tail lowers, the deer has again relaxed and believes everything to be safe.

As a result of not being able to see anything except the ground directly in front of its nose, due to the location of the eyes in the head, when its head is down, a feeding whitetail will raise its head every few seconds to look around and sniff the air. If there is no danger detected, it will flick its tail a couple of times, then resume feeding. The flicking tail means that everything is in order and no danger is present.

The ears of a deer must be watched by the hunter also. If a deer's head is up and its ears are turned forward, it has heard something. At this time the tail will also begin to rise slowly. If the sound can be labeled as natural, the tail will flick and the ears will turn as the deer lowers its head to resume feeding.

Aside from the body signals, the whitetail also communicates through vocal sounds. A loud snort means an uncomfortable deer that senses danger. This snort can be heard for very long distances and will alert any deer in the area. The doe usually does most of the snorting. A buck has a tendency to stand back and let the doe do the scouting and

The upraised white "flag" indicates that this buck is only seconds away from being gone.

signaling, while he thinks of only his own safety, and will either slip away or hide if possible until the danger has passed.

The doe will emit a low bleating grunt when communicating with her fawns or with a buck during the rutting season. Fawns also use this signal to keep track of their mother. A louder bleat, much like that of a goat, means that a deer is in pain and hurting. This sound will sometimes bring other deer to investigate, usually does.

If a hunter has the opportunity, he should study these various signals and if at all possible watch the deer use them before hunting season. A knowledge of these signals and what they mean could make the difference between meat on the table or seeing the white flag.

77

FEEDING AND BEDDING HABITS

As already noted, the whitetail deer usually lives out its life within a square mile of where it was born. In states where dogs are used for chasing deer, a whitetail will return to its home area after the dogs have given up the chase, even when this requires a return trip of several miles. The refusal of whitetails to leave their home range sometimes causes them to starve to death when the area becomes overpopulated and the food supply runs out.

Within the small area where a whitetail makes its home, there are favorite feeding and bedding areas, which are connected by trails or runways that deer use to travel between the two. Except during hunting season, when the deer are pressured, they will travel the same trails daily until the food supply or weather conditions force them to change. They may not travel on the exact trail every time, especially through open woods, but they will travel in the same general area. If they have to traverse heavy undergrowth or outcroppings of rocks, they will usually use the same trail, and it will become a beaten path with old as well as fresh tracks on it.

When hunting season opens and hunters are moving through the area, the deer may change their travel patterns completely, but they seldom change their feeding and bedding habits. This is why some hunters say that a deer is so predictable and easy to hunt. If a good feeding or bedding area can be found, then the chances of finding a deer are very good.

Due to the suspicious nature of the whitetail, they prefer not to expose themselves in open fields or crossways any more than they have to. They do most of their traveling at night and through heavily wooded areas or around the edges of open fields. Grown-up fence rows that separate open fields are favorite travel routes for deer.

Deer will begin to feed about an hour or an hour and a half before dark and will feed until around midnight. At this time they will venture out into open places such as oat fields or orchards. They like to eat just about any type of tender green

Feeding and Bedding Habits

browse and grass and most types of nuts. Their favorite foods will depend on the area where they live.

2½-3"

Trail showing drag marks   Trail showing dewclaws

Tracks of a whitetail deer.

Sometimes around midnight the deer will lie down and chew their cud for a while. Deer, like domestic cattle, have four compartments in their stomach. As they feed, the food is only partially chewed and it goes into the first stomach, known as the rumen, where it is stored until the deer is ready to regurgitate it in small amounts and finish chewing it. This is known as chewing the cud. After the food is rechewed, it is again swallowed into the second stomach, the reticulum, where digestion begins. Before digestion is completed, the food has to pass through the third and fourth stomachs known as the omasum and the abomasum.

Before daylight, the deer has finished chewing its cud and will again be up and feeding, but shortly after sunup it will begin to move toward the daytime bedding area. In flat country, bedding areas are usually found in the thickest sections of the woods, where the deer are most protected. Here, trails leading into the thickets can usually be found. Whenever possible, deer prefer to bed down on the crests of ridges or on hillsides where they can see any movement below them. Also, air currents flowing upwards over the ridges will carry scents of any animal or human to the deer's sensitive nose. The deer can easily slip over the top of the ridge and be gone before any danger approaching from below can reach them.

Although the whitetail will usually bed down in its favorite general areas, it seldom uses exactly the same bed two days in a row. If a hunter finds a deer bed, he can be fairly certain that it is no more than a couple of days old at the most. After a day or two, the grass and leaves that were pressed down by the body of the resting deer will straighten out and remove any indication that a deer slept there. (For a more detailed description of a deer bed, see the section on preseason scouting.)

After bedding down until approximately midday, the whitetail will usually get up and move around for a short time to browse and to relax its muscles. But it won't move very far and will soon bed down again until the time to move toward its nighttime feeding areas.

A severe change in the weather will cause the whitetail to change its feeding pattern. Deer seem to know when bad weather such as a storm is coming, and they try to store up as much food as possible so they can remain in a protected area during the storm. They will be moving at all times of the day just preceding bad weather. Unless the storm lasts for several days, there will be very little deer movement until it is over. After the bad weather has passed, the deer may again be found browsing at any time of the day.

A light rain does not seem to affect the feeding and bedding habits of deer. Their protective coats of hair shed water and even light snow. However, heavy rain and sleet tends to drive them to shelter. A high wind also tends to bother the whitetail. When a strong wind is blowing, deer will be very nervous and skittish. The wind will cause scents to scatter quickly, limbs to fall, leaves to rustle, and brush to crack, all of which makes it hard for a deer to distinguish natural sounds and smells from those made by enemies.

I watched a large doe feeding beneath my tree stand one very windy day for several minutes. She was so nervous that she was actually trembling. Her legs were spread wide and she appeared ready to explode into four directions at once at any moment. There was a fawn with her and she was constantly calling it close to her. Finally, a small twig blew out of the tree and landed about two feet from her nose. She was gone in a flash.

PART IV

THE HUNT

PRESEASON SCOUTING

When we were in school, "homework" was considered to be a dirty word. But for the wise deer hunter, homework before the season begins can mean the difference between getting a deer and not even seeing one. Even if the area to be hunted is the same one a bowhunter has used for several years, he should still start checking it out several weeks in advance of the hunt. Deer may not be moving on the same trails, feeding in the same areas, or bedding down where they did last season, and these are the things that a hunter must know about his game if he plans to be successful. Otherwise, he may spend the entire season sitting on a stand without seeing a deer even though they may be passing within 200 yards of him, just over a ridge, on the other side of a thicket, or across a creek from the spot he has chosen to stand.

In an unfamiliar area, a good way to locate general areas of high deer population is to study the statistics published by the fish and game commissions of most states and compare the hunter-kill ratio for each area. These statistical reports are usually based on certain counties or groups of counties, so the hunter's work has just begun when he decides which county he wants to hunt. A county is a large piece of landscape and must be cut down until a hunter-size area can be established.

The next thing the hunter should do is to talk to local residents and game officials to find out where deer are most often seen crossing highways and backroads or where they are observed feeding. Also, if the hunter lives in a state where there is very little open public land for hunting, he should ask about available leases. After establishing a general idea of where the deer are, the hunter can begin his search.

He should get out into the woods early in the mornings and late in the afternoons, when deer do most of their moving and are more easily spotted traveling to and from their bedding and feeding areas. He should drive the backroads both morning and night, and when he spots a deer he should check out the area carefully, because it may be a regular trail and a hot spot.

If possible, the hunter should climb a tree, a hill, or a fire tower where he can see over a wide area. A good pair of binoculars will be a great aid in spotting deer movement.

Tracks, Scrapes, and Droppings

Once a general picture of the deer movement has been developed, the bowhunter can start the finer points of his pre-season scouting. He should start looking for heavily used trails, tracks, rubs, scrapes, dung, and feeding and bedding areas.

A trail with a lot of tracks in it does not necessarily mean a great deal. If it has not rained recently and there are old and new tracks of various sizes traveling in both directions, then the hunter can be fairly certain that he has found a good trail. By following a trail, the hunter will be able to locate the feeding and bedding areas.

Some old-time deer "experts" say that they can distinguish a buck track from those made by a doe. This ability will help a hunter decide where he should plan his stalk or place his stand. However, it is not a proven fact that the sex of a deer can be told by its track. Big does leave tracks much larger than those of small bucks.

There are a few guidelines a tracker can follow in order to determine if he is tracking a buck or a doe, but he can never be really certain. In most cases, the tracks of a doe are pointed, with the tracks of the hind feet appearing ahead of those left by the forefeet. Also, the tips of the tracks will tend to point straight ahead. The tracks left by a buck are usually more rounded on the tips and the toes appear to turn out rather than point straight ahead as the doe tracks do. A large buck will tend to drag his feet more than a doe, so in light snow or mud a tracker may find drag marks along with the tracks.

The walking track of a heavy deer will show the dewclaw marks and the toes will be spread apart. Of course, the track of a heavy deer does not mean that it is a buck; it could be a fat doe. The running track of both buck and doe will show the dewclaw marks, and the toes will be spread wide apart. So don't let so-called experts tell you that you are tracking a buck just because the dewclaws are showing. The only sure way to tell if the track was left by a buck or a doe is to see the deer that made it!

Fresh tracks in snow show ice or melt in the print. Fresh tracks in mud are still oozing and are sometimes filled with a thin layer of water. New prints on dry ground are sharp around the edges. Old tracks appear to be cast in plaster and are usually eroded at the edges.

As mentioned before, evidence of several tracks does not necessarily indicate the passage of a herd of deer. A very few deer using the same trail daily will leave many tracks. Also, if the hunter is looking for bucks only, doe tracks mean little. Of course, if doe are present there is usually a buck around, but he may not be using the same trails and it would be a waste of time to hunt doe trails for a buck.

There are other ways to determine if a buck is in the area and what trails he is using. Buck rubs along the trails indicate that a buck is using the trail. Lots of fresh rubs are a big help to a hunter planning his tactics for opening day. If scrapes are also found along with rubs and plenty of large tracks, then the hunter can be fairly certain that a large buck is roaming around in the area. A suitable site for a stand can then be chosen.

Besides the rubs, scrapes, and tracks, there are several other sure signs that deer leave for the perceptive hunter. One is dung or droppings, which look much like that of a rabbit except the droppings of a deer are usually darker in color and more oblong in shape.

The size of the pellets will give the hunter an idea of the size of the deer. Here again, the sex of a deer cannot be determined by the droppings even though some people contend that a buck leaves a pellet of a different size and shape than a doe.

The hunter should look for fresh droppings while doing his preseason scouting. Fresh pellets are soft and pliable, but will become hard and brittle after one day. If the sign is not fresh, it means that a deer has not been there recently. If there are both old and fresh droppings, then the deer are visiting the area on a regular basis and the area may be a feeding or bedding area or a trail between the two.

If the area is being used for a bedding ground, the hunter will be able to find beds. A fresh deer bed can be identified by the pressed-down grass approximately three feet long and two feet wide. If a hunter finds a deer bed, he can be fairly certain that the deer will be returning to the same general area daily to bed down, even if it doesn't sleep in exactly the same place.

After the hunter has found a bedding area, he should scout around for fresh tracks and droppings to help him determine the size of the deer and how many are using that particular spot. A lot of old and new sign means that the deer have been sleeping there for a long period of time and will continue to do so unless they are pressured into changing their habits by hunters, weather, or food.

The hunter should scout the trails leading into the bedding grounds to determine the routes taken by the deer when they are leaving and when they are returning. This knowledge will help him to decide where he should take his stand in the mornings when the deer are returning and in the afternoons when they are heading for their feeding grounds. These trails should also be checked for new and old sign. Deer may change their trails and it would be useless to set up a stand along an unused trail.

Food

An experienced hunter will not be satisfied until he has found where the deer are feeding and what they are eating. Of course, the diet of a deer depends on where it lives, much like that of the human. A man living on a seacoast will eat more seafood than a man living in cattle country. If the deer lives in an area where acorns are plentiful, it will eat them, and the wise hunter will check out all of the oak trees in the area to see if deer are visiting them. The same is true of an area where old abandoned apple orchards are abundant. The hunter should check the ground around the trees daily to see if the apples that are falling from the trees are being eaten. If they are, then deer are most likely feeding on them, and the area will be a hot spot when the season opens, if the apples hold out until that time.

Deer also love to browse on farmland crops such as oats, alfalfa, peas, beans, and corn. If the hunter plans to enter a farming area, his best bet is to check around grain fields or orchards. Find a fresh trail leading to one of them and it is almost certain to have deer on it just before sunset.

The bowhunter should not try to cover an entire open field, but should take his stand alongside the trail leading to it. A bow is a short-range weapon and shots over 20 or 30 yards are much too long for the average archer, so it would be useless to try to cover a field that is 100 yards or more across. The trails leading to the fields offer much closer targets.

The time for a bowhunter to select a tree for his stand, if he plans to hunt from a tree, is while doing the preseason scouting. The tree should not be close to the deer trail. It should be to one side, but within easy bow range. The hunter should climb the tree and check for limbs; many good shots are lost because of limbs that are in the way when the archer draws his bow. Also, any small limbs that could deflect an arrow should be cut or tied back with a heavy cord. Any changes made in the appearance of the tree should be made well in advance of deer season, so the deer will be accustomed to them and will pass on down the trail without looking at the tree. (A more detailed discussion of tree stands is covered in the stands and blinds section.)

If there are any waterholes in the area, they should be scouted out to see if the deer are using them. During the wet years deer can get a drink almost anywhere, so they will seldom visit a large body of water, and it would be useless for a hunter to set up a stand near one. However, during dry years deer have to go to the larger waterholes to drink, and trails leading to them make very good spots for stands.

During dry years, the hunter should check out large water holes, such as this one, during preseason scouting.

CLOTHING AND CAMOUFLAGE

Choosing the proper clothing for a deer hunt can be very difficult and must be done with care, or the hunter may find himself freezing to death in clothes that are too light for Colorado mountain hunting, or drowning in his own perspiration in heavy woolen clothes on a hot humid Texas afternoon. The area to be hunted determines the clothing to be worn.

If the hunter has never hunted in the area, he should write to people who live there, if possible, or even to the chamber of commerce of a nearby town. He should find out what temperatures are like during the day and during the night at the time of year he plans to hunt. Then he should plan his clothes according to the information he receives. It is always advisable to carry extra clothes rather than end up with too few, because it is easier to take a coat off than to put one on that is left in a closet 500 miles away.

The choice of clothing weight should be left up to the individual hunter, since he knows if he is cold or hot by nature. The hunter should also keep in mind the type of hunting he will be doing when he plans his wardrobe. If he is planning to sit on a stand, he will need heavier clothing than if he is planning to do a lot of walking.

The color of clothing should depend on the area to be hunted, much like the weight of the clothing. For example, white should be worn only if there is a heavy snow on the ground. Sporting-goods stores and army surplus stores offer camouflage hunting shirts, pants, jackets, and caps that will blend in with the autumn colors of the woods and at the same time help to break up the outline of the hunter's body. Bowhunters have to pay special attention to the type of camouflage they wear, since they will be closer to the deer than a rifle hunter before they can shoot.

Camouflage clothing should be bought well in advance of hunting season and washed several times before opening day. Unfortunately, it has a tendency to shrink, and it is very disturbing, when you are 30 or 40 miles back in the woods, to find that your pants are four inches too short or your shirt is so tight that a full draw on the bow cannot be reached without ripping a seam. Camouflage clothing should be at least one size too large when it is purchased.

One year I bought a pair of camouflage overalls that fitted. After the first washing, I gave them to a smaller friend of mine. After the second washing his wife received them. Now they are too small for her.

Boots or hunting shoes are one of the most important items on a clothing list. They should be comfortable to the wearer, yet rugged in design so that they do not fall apart after getting wet the first time. The soles should be of a non-slip design and stitched to the body of the shoe rather than glued. Even if the boots feel comfortable when they are new, they should be well broken in before hunting season, or the hunter may find himself suffering from foot sores and blisters after the first day in the woods.

A camouflage shirt and pair of pants will cover most of the body. Other exposed areas, such as the hands and the face that will show up in the woods and be spotted by deer, should be covered with mud or one of the many commercial salves used for this purpose. The best colors are black, green, and brown. Some archers use charcoal mixed with face cream, but this is hard to remove if the charcoal gets into the pores of the skin. Many bowhunters prefer to use a face mask or a net to cover their faces. This type of camouflage will also help to keep gnats and flies away from the face on warm days.

ODOR CONTROL

Regardless of the method of hunting a bowhunter plans to use—stalking, driving, sitting in a tree, or sitting on the ground—he must always keep in mind that the human odor will spook a deer before anything else. The hunter may be able to get away with a little noise or a small movement, but let the deer catch his scent and, depending on the situation, the deer will either sneak away undetected or bound off at a very fast pace.

There is no way that the human odor can be completely covered up, but there are several things that a serious bow-hunter can do to help mask his smell. Odor control can be started at home several days before a hunt begins. The clothes that will be worn should be washed well with soap to remove any stale odors that may be left over from the last hunt, or to remove the "new smell" if they have just been purchased. After being washed with soap, they should be washed again in clean water with no soap, to remove the smell of the soap. Dry them outside, and do not hang them back in the house where the smells of toiletries, cigarettes, and cooking can reach them. Some hunters actually roll their hunting clothes up and pack them in a box or bag that contains fresh leaves or vegetation that is natural to the area they plan to hunt. This may seem like it is going a little too far, but for the serious bowhunter, anything he can do to help gain an advantage over his game is worth the effort.

After reaching camp or the point where a hunt is to begin, the hunter should never cook, stand around a camp fire, or work on his car in his hunting clothes. All of these smells are unnatural to whitetails and will put them on the alert even if it does not spook them immediately. Of course, in an area where loggers are in the woods daily cutting logs, deer become accustomed to the smells of camp fires, oil, gasoline, tobacco, and food, but they also associate these smells with man and will avoid them when at all possible.

The word "tobacco" has started many arguments. Should a hunter smoke or not when he is hunting? All hunters have heard time and time again "Do not smoke when you are deer hunting. The deer will pick up the scent and will be gone before you know it." I for one cannot say that this statement is entirely true, because there have been many times when I have had to put out my cigarette to kill a deer. But this doesn't really prove that cigarette smoking is all right. It just proves that the deer either did not smell the smoke or they failed to react to the smell in time. If a person does not smoke at all or can refrain from the use of tobacco while hunting, then he should.

A serious bowhunter will not wash with soap or use any type of toiletries while on a hunting trip. The smell of shaving creams, deodorant soaps, and after-shave lotions may help to attract a "dear," but not a deer. I'm not saying that a hunter shouldn't take a bath. Of course he should, but in clean fresh water without the use of a deodorant-type soap.

As a hunter stalks through the woods, sits on a stand, or moves to and from his stand, he spreads a trail of human odor. There are many commercial "buck lures" and "odor masks" on the market to help cover up this trail, but the hunter should be very careful which one he chooses to use. For example, he should not use an apple-scented lure if he plans to hunt in a clump of cedars, or a cedar-scented lure if he plans to hunt for deer in an apple orchard.

Most experienced bowhunters agree that probably the best mask, even if not the most pleasant one for the hunter, is skunk musk. A cotton ball saturated with skunk musk and tied to the undersole of a hunter's boot will help to cover up his trail as he moves through the woods. This may make the hunter a little unpopular with his wife or girl friend when he returns home, but if he brings in a big ole buck, they probably won't really mind all that much.

All of these suggestions are helpful for covering up a hunter's smell, but the most important thing he should remember is the wind direction. Try to keep the wind from blowing toward the deer. If stalking, walk into the wind either directly or quarter across it. If sitting on a stand, try to choose one where the wind will be blowing away from the most likely spot for deer movement.

These tips on odor control may not guarantee the hunter a deer, but they will help him to stack the odds in his favor—and that is very important when hunting the wily whitetail.

METHODS OF BOWHUNTING

There are many ways to bowhunt the whitetail, and the region of the country where the hunt is taking place usually dictates, at least in part, the type of hunting to be done. In some states dogs are used for driving deer, while in other states dogs are illegal and men do the driving. States such as Texas allow hunting from tree stands while others forbid it or put a limit on how high the stand can be from the ground. Many hunters like to sit on the ground and wait for a deer to come along and others get out into the woods and stalk them.

Stalking

Stalking is one of the most difficult and most personally rewarding methods of bowhunting the whitetail deer. If the hunter has done his preseason scouting well, he knows where the deer are sleeping, eating, and watering, and where they are most likely to be found at any particular time of the day or night. He knows where the major trails, crossways, buck rubs, and scrapes are, and whether the deer are using them on a regular basis. Then on opening day of the season he is ready to match his bow and woodsmanship against the deer's nose, ears, eyes, and ability to elude its enemies.

Believe me, this is quite a challenge even for a gun hunter who has to get within about 200 yards for an easy shot, but for the bowhunter who must be within 40 yards of the deer, and preferably much less, the challenge seems almost impossible. Yet each year hundreds of bowhunters, old-timers as well as beginners, bring big beautiful bucks out of the woods. They have either done their homework well or were just lucky, or both.

An old saying goes, "A long trip begins with a single step." So does a long stalk. Even though the archer knows where the deer should be, he must find them first, the wind must be in his favor, the deer must be relaxed, and many other factors must be under the control of the hunter or he will never be able to send his arrow into the vital parts of a buck.

The only way to find, approach, and shoot a deer in its own home range is to take one or two slow steps at a time, stop, stay downwind, watch everything that moves, makes a sound, or looks out of place, then take another few steps. Stalking is a very slow way to hunt, but if the hunter is out there to be successful, he must go slow. If he is out there to rush through the woods, he may as well leave his bow at home, because the deer will be long gone before he gets within bow range.

On the day of the hunt, the hunter should arrive at the starting place early and be ready to go as soon as he can see. He should not try to take more equipment or clothing than is absolutely needed, since he will be walking for a long period of time and any additional weight will tend to tire him out sooner. All that he really needs is a bow, arrows, a knife, a short length of rope, something to eat, and a compass if the area is unfamiliar to him. A snake-bite kit is handy if the area to be hunted is still warm enough for poisonous snakes to be out. Bowhunting season comes early enough that it is still very warm in many of the southern states.

Also, before leaving home or camp, someone should be told where the hunt is taking place and approximately what time the hunter will return. These are safety steps that could save a lone hunter his life in case he has an accident or becomes lost.

The Indians were great hunters not because of the weapons they carried, but because of their ability to stalk their game. Modern archers have a great advantage over the Indians in bows and arrows, but their woodsmanship is far below that of the ancient hunters. Indians were trained from childhood to slip quietly through the woods in pursuit of game, since their ability to bring home meat meant the difference between being well fed and going hungry.

The way the hunter walks is very important for being able to slip quietly through the woods. Indians walked on the balls of their feet with the toes pointing straight ahead. This allowed them to feel the ground for twigs and leaves before putting their weight down on the heel of the foot. Today's hunter places the heel of the foot down first then slaps the ball forward, breaking twigs and leaves and scraping gravel with each step. Of course, it is impossible for today's hunter to walk like a white man all year long, then like an Indian during deer season, but it is important to make as little noise as possible. A pair of heavy wool socks worn over the hunting boots will help to cut down on noise.

If a twig should happen to snap, all is not lost, because an unalarmed deer may interpret the sound as being natural since twigs do get broken by other animals and by deer themselves. Just stand completely still for several minutes, then continue on your way.

Although it is necessary to watch the ground for noise-makers, the bowhunter should not spend all his time looking at the ground or he will never see a deer. After a step or two, the stalker should stop, study the woods in front, to the side, and in back of him, plan his next step or two, then move ahead again.

Besides a deer's own senses that warn it of danger, the other animals and birds of the forest act as an alarm system when any strange being enters their home. A whitetail is very sensitive to the sounds made by other animals and birds when an intruder is around. The scolding squirrel or bluejay can warn the deer that a stranger is near even before it smells, sees, or hears the stalker, so the hunter has to be very careful not to disturb the other animals and birds as he moves through the woods. If he does cause a disturbance, he should stop for a few minutes before continuing his stalk.

Many chances to bag a deer are lost because the bowhunter looks but does not see. In other words, he looks at the woods and all he sees is woods, whereas if he knew what to look for he could in many cases see deer where they appear not to be.

Nature has provided the whitetail with a natural ability to camouflage itself in almost any type of cover. Yet a trained eye can spot a deer in the best hiding places.

The novice hunter expects to see the whole deer standing broadside in the classical position whereas the experienced bowhunter knows that a chance like that comes only a few times in a lifetime. He looks for parts of the deer, because that is all there is to see in most cases. In good deer country, the undergrowth is usually a tangled mixture of briars, sprouts, bushes, and low-hanging limbs, so anything symmetrical should be checked out. It could be an eye, ear, or nose of a deer. Also, most lines are vertical in the woods, so the stalker should always look for horizontal lines that may be the back of a deer that is hiding and waiting for the hunter to pass by, which is a common practice of wise deer.

The stalker should also be alert for small patches of white that could be the throat of a deer, or for a black spot that could be its nose. He should also check out any movement he may see, since it may be a deer's tail or ear twitching.

As the hunter slips through the woods, being constantly alert for sounds, movements, and parts of a deer, he should

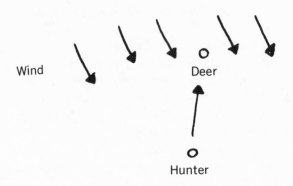

The stalker should always move into the wind.

always be conscious of the wind direction. He should always face or quarter into the wind. It is very seldom that a hunter successfully stalks a deer that is downwind from him. The deer will smell him and be gone in a flash.

A wise hunter will watch his back trail as well as ahead of him. If a deer knows something is following it, it will often circle behind or downwind in order to catch the smell of the pursuer. When the hunter thinks he has been spotted, he should backtrack a couple hundred yards and wait. The wily whitetail may outsmart itself and circle into an ambush. As mentioned earlier, whitetails usually bed down along the tops of a ridge or any high place that will offer them a good view of anything below them. The wise stalker will thus plan his stalk along the tops of ridges, so he will be above and behind the deer.

A bowhunter's work has just begun when a deer is spotted. He must now get within bow range without being detected, and that can be a tremendous task. First of all, he should check the area carefully for other deer. They usually travel in twos or more except for bucks during the rut, and this can cause the careless stalker to lose his chance even if the deer he is concentrating on never detects his presence. Another deer may spot the hunter and give the alarm, so the careful stalker must locate all of the deer and watch each of them as he moves in on his target.

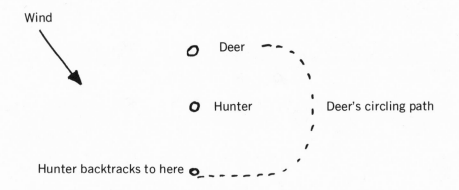

Backtrack if you feel the deer has seen you and often you can ambush it.

If possible, it is more practical to watch the deer for a few minutes to see which direction they are moving, then circle them and set up an ambush. If wind direction or other factors prevent this move, the hunter must slip in very slowly using every precaution not to disturb the deer. He should move only when the deer is facing away from him or has its head down. When a deer's head is down, it can see only the ground in front of its nose, due to the location of its eyes.

A deer knows that it is most vulnerable when its head is down, so it does not browse very long without bringing its head up for a look around. If all is well, it will lower its head in a few seconds and resume eating. There have been hunters who could slip up to within 10 or 15 steps of a feeding deer without being detected.

The main factors to remember when stalking a deer are to go slowly, face the wind, move only when the deer is not looking, and aim carefully when taking the shot, because in most cases there will be time for only one.

Tree Stands and Blinds

Probably the most practical and productive type of hunting for the whitetail with a bow and arrow is from a tree stand or a

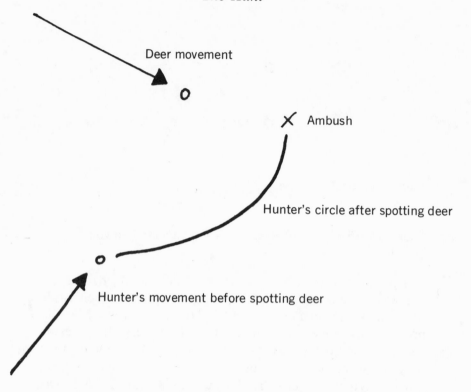

Deer movement

Ambush

Hunter's circle after spotting deer

Hunter's movement before spotting deer

A wise stalker will sometimes circle moving deer and set up an ambush rather than try to move in on them.

blind. Today's bowhunters, for the most part, are not skilled enough in woodsmanship and deer know-how to be able to stalk a deer close enough for a good bow shot. Sitting in a tree or a blind can be their answer for a successful hunt.

Just finding a good tree and climbing up in it is not all there is to hunting from a tree. The location of the stand must be chosen with care, or you may find yourself sitting on a limb all day with nothing to show for it but a sore backside.

Preseason scouting is very important to the stand hunter. The site chosen for a stand must offer concealment, yet be within easy bow range of where the deer are moving on a regular basis. If you are fortunate enough to find an acorn, apple, or other type of tree where deer are feeding, then you have a perfect place for a stand. Otherwise, you must find a well-used trail or a place where several trails come together, and build your stand there.

The stand itself should be as close to the trail as possible without disturbing the deer as they pass by. Often a hunter in a tree will have a deer feed directly beneath him without detecting his presence. As long as he is well camouflaged, does not move or make a sound, and the deer does not catch his scent, he will usually go unnoticed. Even if the deer should happen to look at him, if he remains motionless, they will not usually become alerted.

Those "experts" also say that deer never look up. Once again, they're wrong. Deer *will* look up especially if they sense the presence of danger from above. It is true that by nature whitetail deer seldom look up, but should the hunter in a tree stand make even the slightest noise he will look straight into the eyes of a deer.

The fact that deer seldom look up unless disturbed is only one advantage a tree sitter has over the hunter who stays on the ground. Movement is less readily detected when you are above the normal vision of the deer. Also, your odor will be carried away above the animals unless it is a very cold, still day. Cold air, being heavier than warm air, will settle to the ground, carrying the human odor with it unless there is a breeze to lift it up and move it away.

A wise stand hunter will choose several possible sites, since wind direction may change, making a stand useless at certain times of the day. For example, if deer are traveling north to a feeding ground and the wind is blowing toward the southwest, then the hunter should station himself on the west side of the trail. This is an oversimplified example, but from it you can get an idea of how wind direction will affect your standing position.

Another reason for having several sites prescouted is that deer may use different trails when going to and from a feeding area. The same holds true for bedding areas. A good morn-

The Hunt

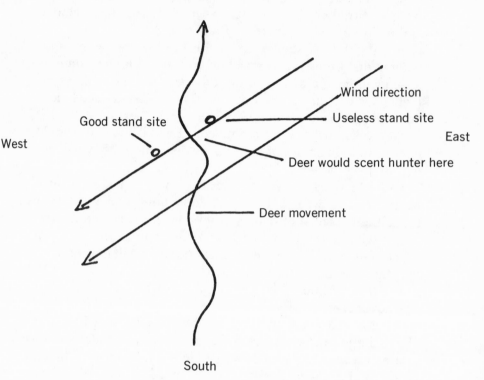

North

Wind direction

Useless stand site

Good stand site

West

East

Deer would scent hunter here

Deer movement

South

Wind direction is an important factor when choosing a stand site.

ing stand could turn out to be no good at all in the afternoon.

Still another reason for choosing several locations is the possibility that the deer may spot your stand and avoid it. One good example of this happened to a friend of mine, Jim Hoedebeck, while we were bowhunting in central Texas one season.

We always sit on our stands until almost dark, so we have to carry a flashlight with us in order to see how to get back to camp without stepping on a rattlesnake or falling into a cactus bed. One afternoon, just as it was beginning to get dark, Jim noticed a young buck looking straight up into his tree through the branches of a cedar bush about 25 yards out. Jim could not understand how the buck had spotted him so easily, since he had been sitting perfectly still, was well camouflaged, and had the wind in his favor. Nevertheless, there was the buck peeping through the cedar bush directly at him.

You may have already guessed it—Jim's flashlight was on! When he had stuck it into his pocket, the switch had caught and turned the light on. It was just dark enough for the beam of light to attract the young buck's attention to Jim's tree. Disgruntled, Jim climbed down from the tree, stomped back to camp, and sheepishly told his tale to an amused audience.

The next morning, Jim was again in his tree at daybreak and the young buck was again behind the cedar bush peeping through the branches at Jim. Jim had been spotted! Even though he is an excellent marksman with a bow, he cannot hit what he cannot see and there was just no way that deer was going to move out from behind that bush as long as Jim was there.

While Jim sat patiently watching his deer stare at him, he noticed that directly behind the cedar bush that concealed the buck was another large oak tree within bow range. Jim decided that he could shoot that smart "son of a doe" with no problem from that tree.

That afternoon, Jim was sitting in the new tree and when the young buck came calling, he received an arrow through his right shoulder as he peeped through the cedar bush at an empty tree.

There are several disadvantages to hunting from a tree, such as limited shooting space and limbs that seem to be in exactly the wrong place when a deer walks by. Tree sitters should use a safety rope in case they slip while in their stands. A fall from 12 to 15 feet could ruin a good hunting trip, to say the least. A stout rope tied around the shoulders will prevent this and at the same time give the hunter stability when he shoots.

As far as the type of stand that should be used, there are any number of good ones. The location of the stand and the state and local regulations concerning tree stands should be considered before building the stand. Many states do not allow elevated stands at all while others allow them if they are portable and not left in the tree. Still other states allow permanent stands to be built with boards and nails.

Elevated stands range all the way from a single board laid across a tree limb to elaborate structures with heaters and sliding windows. Take your pick! I personally prefer to find a tree where I can stand or sit on one limb and lean back against the tree trunk. From this position I find it easier to move without too much commotion if a deer should come up on my "off-side," which they invariably do.

Hunters who prefer to be on the ground rather than in an elevated stand must choose their site with as much care as tree sitters, if not more. They will be at eye level with the deer and will thus be more detectable.

If the hunter's body outline is broken up by a good background such as high grass or thick brush, then he is fairly well hidden. The deer may see him but fail to interpret him as being a danger. A hollowed-out clump of brush or fallen tree can make a very good stand if the outside is not disturbed, because the deer will see the brush as they always have, while the hunter is sitting comfortably inside. Camouflage netting also offers very good concealment for the stander. A ground blind should be built high enough to conceal the bowhunter, but allow him to shoot over it without too much movement when getting into a shooting position.

Comfort is another thing that should be considered when choosing a stand, whether it is in a tree or on the ground. The stander must remember that he will be there for several hours without moving anymore than necessary, so he must be comfortable. A small foam cushion or a portable stool is very handy and can provide a lot of comfort over the hours.

Regardless of the type stand a hunter chooses, he should remember a few important facts. The stand should be within bow range of heavy deer traffic, it must be downwind of the direction deer will be traveling, it should provide maximum concealment and comfort without alerting the deer, and the route to the stand should be well known to the hunter so he

Well-constructed permanent stands such as this one are used mainly by gun hunters.

can find it before daylight without too much wandering around. The less he walks around in the area, the less human scent he will distribute.

The most important factor a good stand hunter should remember is to get into a shooting position while the deer is not looking in his direction. Wait until the deer lowers its head or has it behind a bush, before drawing the bow. If the deer is looking at the hunter when the arrow is released, it will often move faster than the arrow and get out of the way before it reaches its mark. However, if the deer is looking away when the arrow is released, it is more likely to hesitate that fraction of a second longer that will allow the arrow to reach its mark in time for a good solid hit.

Baiting a Stand

Many bowhunters consider baiting a stand to be taking an undue advantage of the deer. However, many other bowhunters believe that any edge they can get is in order, since man is really not a match for a whitetail when it comes to woods know-how. The deer is better equipped than is a hunter, so getting the deer to come in for a close shot is all part of the game in many bowhunting circles.

If a bowhunter decides to bait his stand, he should first check with the local authorities to be sure there is no ordinance against it. A telephone call to the game warden's office will only take a few minutes and it could save the hunter a fine if there is a law against baiting in that area.

Baiting should be started well in advance of opening day, so the deer will know where the food is and will stop by for it on a daily schedule. The bait should be easy to handle for the hunter and well liked by the deer. Many hunters have read that apples are the favorite food of the whitetail and that the deer will travel miles to get one. This may be true in locations where apple trees are plentiful, but what about areas where the only apples around are in someone's lunch sack? The deer in those areas have never tasted one, so they do not know what it offers and will not be drawn to a stand by them.

Grain is a favorite bait used in many states. The hunter can carry it to the stand and put it out without ever touching the grain itself with his hands. If he does touch it, there is always the possibility that some wise old deer will smell the human scent left on it and refuse to eat.

If grain is to be used for bait, it should be scattered in a wide circle around the stand, for the first few feedings. The circle should extend out away from the stand for as much as 50 to 60 yards. Then, as opening day draws nearer, the circle should be brought in gradually to about 20 to 30 yards from the stand in order to offer the best possible shots for the hunter. For the last feeding before opening day and for feedings after the season has begun, the grain should be placed only in spots where the archer can be sure of a well-placed shot. It would be a waste of feed to put it behind a bush or tree where the hunter could not see the deer, much less shoot at it.

A grain feeder can be very useful when baiting a stand. It will feed out small amounts of grain, which will cut down on waste and loss to birds and other animals. The grain feeder is not a natural thing found in the woods and as the grain falls out there is some noise, so it should be placed on or near the stand well in advance of deer season, so the deer will grow accustomed to its presence and purpose.

Some bowhunters have said that when deer are in the area and hear the grain falling out of the feeder, they will come in to eat after they have learned what causes the noise. This may or may not be true, but it does seem possible.

A good grain feeder can be constructed by the hunter for very little money and time. All that is needed is a clean five-gallon bucket with a bail and lid, two large funnels, a length of wire (coat hanger), and a $1^{1}/_{2}$-inch bolt with a nut. The following photos show how simple it is to put a feeder together.

Driving with Dogs and Men

Deer drives have been a part of deer hunting for many years and can be very productive, even for a bowhunter. As a rule, bowhunters prefer to stalk their deer or use a blind, since the majority of shots during a drive will be at fast-moving targets. Gun hunters have the advantage of longer range and faster moving projectiles, so they can use the drive with a greater amount of success than the bowhunter. However, if a drive is handled properly, bowhunters can take home trophies.

A well-organized drive will have standers placed at all of the known trails used by deer during their daily movements from feeding to bedding areas. Someone has to do quite a lot of preseason scouting in order to find these trails and know where to place the standers. Otherwise, a drive may be completed without a single deer being seen.

There are countless variations for making a deer drive, but most of them fall into three major categories: driving with

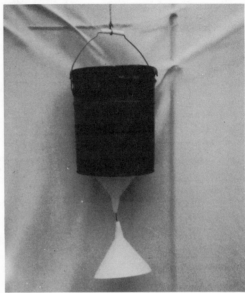

These items and about thirty minutes of your time are all that is needed to build a good grain feeder.

dogs, driving with men who are acting as beaters and making as much noise as possible, and driving with men who are silently moving through the woods. The first two categories are used mainly by gun hunters. The use of dogs began in Europe where hunting with dogs and horses was a great sport enjoyed by the nobility. Later the use of dogs spread to America where it is still practiced in many states, while it has been outlawed in others.

For a successful dog drive, there must be several hunters who take up stands along a line in front of the drive. These standers usually know from past experience where the deer will most likely cross out when the dogs are after them, and in many cases the same man will hunt a certain spot year after year. Newcomers to the group have to find their own spots or take ones vacated by old-timers who are not hunting.

At a given time, a driver will take the dogs into the woods and try to strike a fresh deer trail. When a trail is struck, he turns the dogs loose and the hunt is under way. Hopefully, the dogs will be after a buck and take it out by some lucky stander.

Often a buck being chased by dogs will join with one or several does, then at the right moment he will take a long jump to one side and let the dogs continue on after the does. The buck will then try to slip out of the area or conceal himself in a thicket until the drive is over and the danger has passed.

Most whitetails that are being pursued by dogs will move by the standers at a very fast pace, and if the hunter is not alert he will miss his chance for a shot. That is one reason why bowhunters are at a disadvantage when dogs are used on a drive.

Some old-timers enjoy a good dog drive for the excitement of listening to the chase. They do not care if they see a deer or not, just as long as the dogs put on a good show.

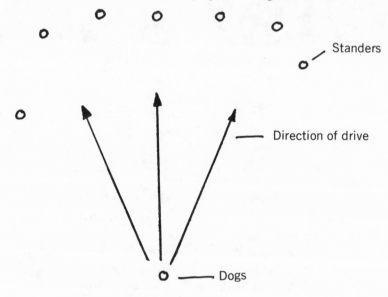

A typical drive using dogs.

In states where the use of dogs is not permitted, hunters take their places and move through the woods, beating the brush and making as much noise as possible. Hopefully this will serve two purposes—to drive the deer toward the standers and to prevent someone from taking a shot at one of the drivers, thinking he is a deer. This does not happen as often with bowhunters as with gun hunters, but there have been cases where a careless bowhunter shot an arrow at another hunter.

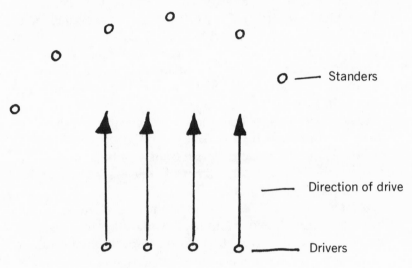

A typical drive using men instead of dogs.

A smart whitetail can usually avoid the drivers and standers by choosing a spot between the noisy men and either slipping by them or laying down in the brush until the men have passed by and it is safe to move again.

I remember one hunt in Arkansas that my cousin, Pug White, loves to tell about. He and several of his friends have used dogs for many years to drive deer, but one year for some reason they did not have enough dogs for a good drive, so some of the men agreed to become "dogs for a day." They gathered up old dish pans, pots, and other items that would make a noise, and set out through the woods raising as much commotion as possible. The deer in that area were used to dogs and knew how to elude them, but this was something new and confusing to them, so they just ran. Pug says that he has never seen so many deer on one drive before. They went crazy with fear and ran in every direction. I do not remember how many deer he said were killed that day, but everyone had a full day of hunting.

The silent drive can be successful for bowhunters if handled properly. This type of drive is organized and carried out in the same manner as the noisy drive except that the men doing the driving make as little noise as possible. They actually slip through the woods as if they were stalking the deer rather than trying to drive them. Although there are times when the driver is able to get within bow shot and score a deer himself, the purpose of the silent drive is to move the deer toward the standers without alarming them.

If the deer are not spooked, they will usually move ahead of the drivers along their regular trails. A stander who happens to be on a stand near one of those trails will be able to get a shot at a slow-moving deer, unless the deer sees the stander first and circles around him.

Two men can carry out a drive if they go about it in the proper way. As shown by the following diagram, the first driver moves slowly through the area to be hunted while a second hunter follows him a couple hundred yards back. If a deer feels that it is being pursued, it may circle around and try to come up behind the hunter. Often this will give the second hunter a nice shot.

As mentioned earlier, driving is less popular with bowhunters than stalking or blind hunting, yet after two or three days of walking until your feet are numb or sitting until your backside is calloused, you may be ready for a good drive. If there are two or more hunters in the party, then organize a drive. It may surprise you!

Rattling and Calling

Mention "rattling up a buck" in most hunting circles, and south Texas comes to mind. That is where rattling is supposed to have originated and been used successfully for many years. But the art of beating a couple of deer antlers together

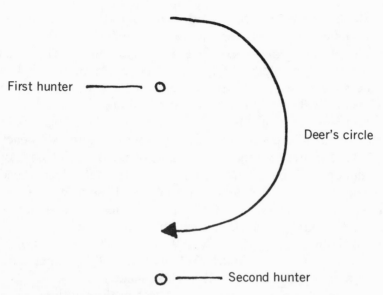

First hunter

Deer's circle

Second hunter

A two-man drive.

to call in a buck can be used anywhere during the rutting season of the whitetail deer.

During the rutting season, the whitetail buck is very jealous of this territory, and the presence of another buck will usually set him off in a fit of temper. That is the purpose of rattling: to bring in the buck that has staked out a particular area as his private property. When he hears what sounds like two bucks fighting and pushing each other around, he assumes that both of them are trespassing, and he usually comes in closer to investigate.

Some bucks will rush in with hackles raised and blood in their eyes, ready to fight. Others will be a bit more cautious and sneak in or circle the sound trying to get downwind before coming in, so the hunter should be on the alert at all times, and ready for a quick shot.

It is best to have two hunters present—one to do the rattling and one ready to do the shooting. When the buck comes in, he is already alert and tense, so any movement on the hunter's part as he changes from horns to bow will be detected and the deer will be gone in a flash.

Making a pair of rattling antlers is not a difficult job if you have a nice set of eight- or ten-point antlers around the house. Some rattling experts say that the horns must be matched (from the same deer) while others believe that unmatched antlers are best. Both types have been used successfully, so who can really be sure which is the best?

To make a set of rattling antlers, cut off the sharp tips of each tine, the brow points, and any knobs or bumps on each antler. Be sure to smooth the rough edges down with a file or sandpaper. If the antlers were removed from the deer's head above the knurls, drill a hole through the base of each antler and tie them together with a strip of leather, so they can be carried around the neck or over the shoulder without being lost or knocking together as you walk. If they were removed below the knurl, the knurl itself will keep the leather strip from slipping off and no hole will be needed.

That is all there is to making a set of rattling antlers. The rest of the job of calling in a buck is technique. Most old hands at rattling up bucks agree that the following technique is very successful, especially when done on a cold, crisp, wind-less morning.

While preseason scouting, find a spot that offers plenty of camouflage without the deer having to come out into the open. A wise buck seldom crosses an open area, but will tend to keep to the brush while coming in to the sound of the rattling.

If possible, choose a spot that has a rough-barked tree, gravel, and a small bush nearby. A fresh scrape or rub within bow range may also prove helpful, because that means that a buck is roaming the area.

To create the desired sound, hold an antler in each hand with the tines facing each other. Hit them together hard to simulate two bucks banging their heads together. Rattle them a few times, then scrape the gravel, beat on the bush, and rake the tree.

The hunter should not rattle continuously. He should go through all of the actions one or two times, then wait for a few minutes before starting again. If no buck has responded to

Using a pair of antlers to "rattle" up a buck.

the rattling after 20 or 30 minutes, the hunter should move to a new spot, preferably one that has already been checked out, so he can go directly to it without having to spend any time looking for a new place.

Odor control is very important when rattling up a buck. The deer will already have you pinpointed as soon as you start to rattle, and any smell of human odor will certainly cause them considerable concern and will usually keep them away.

Rattling has been a proven method for getting deer to come to the hunter for many years. Another not so well-proven method is "calling" deer with mouth-blown instruments or electrical devices. Since deer are not very vocal animals, it is difficult to produce a sound that will consistently attract them as does rattling.

Most vocal sounds that are made by deer are low grunting noises and these are usually made by fawns in search of their mothers or by does when they are looking for their fawns or for a buck during rutting season. Aside from the grunting sounds, deer occasionally bleat much like a goat, which usually indicates that they are hurting and in extreme pain. So as you can see, the hunter who plans to call a deer has all of the odds stacked against him. Not only does he have very few sounds to imitate, he can also very easily scare the deer away by making the wrong sound.

There are commercial deer calls on the market that are used like duck and varmint calls. Sometimes a few low bleats on one of these will produce deer, but not as consistently as rattling antlers. It is my suggestion that if a hunter plans to use either of the two methods, he should rattle. Also, before trying to call a deer, the hunter should check the local laws. It is unlawful to call deer in some states.

PART V

THE KILL

WHEN AND WHERE TO SHOOT

By now the bowhunter has probably spent quite a lot of time and effort practicing with his bow, studying the whitetail habits, and scouting the areas where he plans to hunt. He has also spent some money on a bow, arrows, accessories, and clothing. All of this time, effort, and expense will seem worthwhile when the hunter spots a beautiful whitetail buck out in front of him on some early morning or late afternoon of the deer season. But unless the hunter has also given some thought to the questions of when he should shoot and where he should place the shot, everything else will have been in vain.

It is not easy to tell a bowhunter exactly when he should shoot because there are so many variables to be considered for each deer. The hunter never knows what to expect when he is trying to outwit a whitetail. He must make up his own mind when to shoot and where to aim, but he must also have a pretty good idea before the deer appears.

Usually a close shot is better, but the hunter must remember that the closer he is to the deer, the better chance the deer has of catching the scent or seeing the movement of the hunter. A deer can hear the string noise and move quickly enough to keep the arrow from hitting him.

The bowhunter should have a very good knowledge of a whitetail's anatomy. As shown in the illustration, most of the vital organs of a deer are in the front half of the body, and that is where the bowhunter should try to place his arrow. However, that isn't always easy. The deer in the illustration is standing broadside in order to show the location of various organs, but the deer a hunter sees in the woods will rarely be standing broadside. Therefore, angle shots must be practiced before opening day.

The average bowhunter should choose a point of aim behind the shoulder blade and about midway between the back and belly line of the deer. This aiming point allows for some error. A high shot may still hit the lungs, a low one may hit the heart or liver.

119

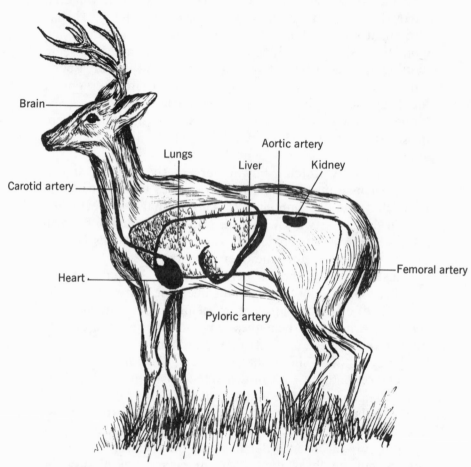

Deer anatomy.

A hit in the lungs will usually bring a deer down within 100 to 200 yards. If you have studied animal anatomy, you know that death is caused by drowning when the lungs are filled with liquid. That is what happens when a broadhead passes through the lungs; they fill with blood and the deer actually drowns. The blood trail left by a deer hit in the lungs will be very bright red and frothy. A good hit in the lungs will cause a lot of bleeding, which makes trailing much easier.

A heart shot is more difficult to make than a lung shot, due to the heart's smaller size and its location in the deer's body. But a heart shot is a very fatal shot, and the deer will usually move less than 100 yards after being hit. The blood will be a deep red color and will be in spurts due to the pumping action of the heart.

Liver shots will not produce as much bleeding as lung or heart shots, but they will put a deer down fairly soon. The blood will be a dark red and in smaller drops than found in lung and heart shots.

Kidney hits are also good since they cause a lot of bleeding and the more a deer bleeds, the sooner it will weaken and lie down.

Other highly effective hits are spine and brain shots, which almost always put the deer down where it is hit. It's not recommended that a beginning bowhunter try for brain shots. They are very difficult and offer such a small target that it is almost impossible for anyone less than a champion archer to hit the brain, especially under the nervous strain the hunter is in when shooting at a deer. Spine shots are not as difficult as brain shots and when the hunter is in a tree stand or elevated above the deer, the chances are fair that his arrow will pass through the spine on its downward path to the chest cavity.

The artery system of a deer is its life line, just as in any other mammal. Large amounts of blood are continuously circulating through this system, and anytime an artery is severed, the deer will bleed out fairly soon and leave an easy trail to follow.

Neck shots are good for rifle hunters, due to the shocking effect of the expanding bullet, but since an arrow depends on hemorrhage to kill, neck shots are not recommended for the bowhunter. True, the spine, windpipe, and carotid arteries run through the neck, but they offer a very small target, and unless one of them is cut, the deer will receive only a painful and non-fatal flesh wound.

The paunch or stomach area is the largest part of a deer, but it is the least fatal. A paunch- or "gut"-shot deer bleeds very little and often requires hours before it dies. The trail, if there is any, will have particles of undigested food and a greenish-yellow matter mixed with the blood.

A hit in any one or a combination of the preceding vital areas will kill a deer. It would be nice if we could stop at this point and say to the bowhunter, "Study the anatomy drawing and you will know where to hit your deer," but it is not that easy, because a deer must be approached in ways other than broadside. Angle shots place a new perspective on the location of vital areas in regard to the hunter's point of aim.

The most difficult shots to make are when the deer is standing head on or quartering in toward the hunter. Not only is the target small, but the deer is more likely to see any movement a bowhunter makes as the bow is drawn.

When a deer is facing the hunter head on, he has two possible targets. If the range is fairly close, the hunter can aim at the white spot on the deer's neck. From this angle, the broadhead will most likely sever the windpipe, carotid artery, and spine. The hunter must keep in mind that this is a very small target and the shot should not be attempted unless he feels sure that he can hit it.

The other choice is lower in the chest. A hit in this area will cut through the heart or lungs, or both, unless the arrow is deflected by the ribs that come together at this point. If the bowhunter is in a tree, the head-on or quartering-in angles are really tough. With a downward angle, the arrow is more likely to be deflected by the ribs and do no real damage. Try to wait until the deer lowers its head, then aim at the point between the shoulder blades where the neck joins the shoulders. A hit here will break the spine or will penetrate the lungs if it misses the spine.

The rear-end shot is not the most desirable shot, but can be effective. If arrow penetration is good, the arrow will pass through to the heart and lung area, possibly cutting the

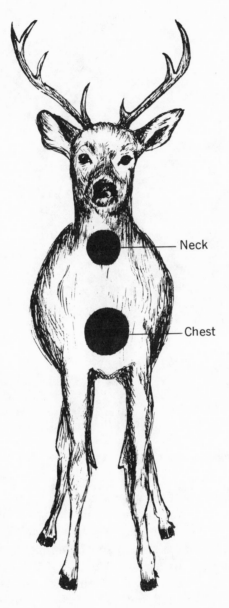

Neck

Chest

Head-on angle.

Quartering-in angle.

kidneys as it passes. If the hunter is elevated, the arrow may cut the spine on its way to the lungs. Another thing to remember is the deer cannot see the hunter make his draw from this angle. I once had a rear-in shot at a nice six-point buck from a tree stand. I overshot my aim, but the arrow caught the deer at the base of the skull, which cut his spine away from his head and downed him on the spot. Needless to say, I was very surprised.

The most effective shot is the quartering-away angle. The arrow should be placed just behind the near shoulder, so it

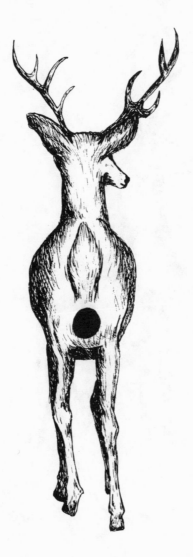

Rear-end angle.

Quartering-away angle.

angles forward toward the front of the opposite shoulder.
The lungs, heart, and liver will be severed and the deer will
not travel far before it will lie down to rest and in most cases
die.

Regardless of the angle, if the tree-stand hunter will keep in
his mind the top view of a deer shown here, he will be able to
determine where the arrow should be placed for maximum
killing effect. A word to the wise: If a deer is coming head on
and has not seen you, try to wait until it passes your stand before making your shot.

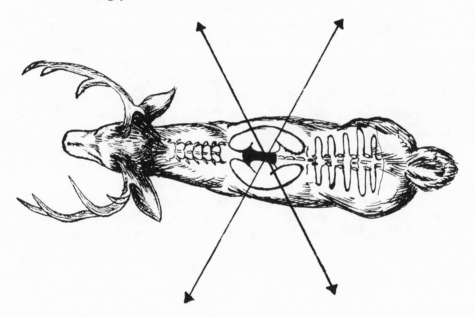

Top view.

BUCK FEVER

Buck fever can strike any hunter whether he be an experienced deer killer or a novice who has never seen a deer in the
woods. It often occurs just as the hunter is drawing down on
a big old buck. First his arms begin to shake, then his knees,

then his breathing becomes heavy and rapid, and sometimes he may even break out in a cold sweat. As a result, the buck usually gets away and the hunter becomes the target for many jokes from his hunting partners. If this should ever happen to you, don't be overly concerned because most of the hunters who will make fun of you have already had their turn and will probably have it again someday.

There is no sure cure for buck fever, because it is a result of the excitement of seeing a big buck and the fear of letting it get away. If there is time, the archer should try to relax, breathe deeply, and tell himself that it is only a deer and there is nothing to be lost even if it gets away, except maybe a wall trophy and something to brag about. He should watch the deer for a few minutes until his arms quit shaking, then try again. The arrows should not be released as long as the arms are shaking, since that could result in a badly aimed shot and a wounded deer that may run for miles before it dies.

Some experts recommend that exposure to deer works as a preventive for the fever, but I have seen and killed many fine deer in the past and I still have a touch of it at times. Of course, a slight nervousness does not mean that the hunter has buck fever. That is a normal condition among deer hunters, caused by the excitement. Some old-timers say that if they ever fail to become excited when they see a deer, it will be time for them to quit hunting. Once the excitement is gone, so is the fun.

TRAILING WOUNDED DEER

Let us assume that a bowhunter has shot a deer and feels fairly certain that his aim was true and a hit was made. What does he do now? There have been many controversial articles written about the next steps to take, but they all agree that the deer should be followed and recovered if at all possible. No sportsman would fail to do his best to find a wounded deer.

Trailing Wounded Deer

How *soon* the deer should be followed has caused many hours of heated discussion among hunters without a definite answer being resolved. There are so many variables for each situation, but the consensus seems to be that the hunter should not jump up immediately after a hit and take off after the wounded deer. Rather, he should watch it until it disappears into the brush, then make mental notes of landmarks near the last sighting, where the deer was standing when hit, and at what angle to the archer it was standing. Knowing the probable area of its anatomy where the deer was hit will determine how soon the trail should be taken up.

Often the deer will give some visible reaction when hit that may clue the hunter to where the arrow was placed in the body. A plunging leap with the forelegs tucked close to the chest may mean a heart shot. If the deer humps up in the middle, the hunter can assume a hit in the paunch. A limping or staggering deer indicates a serious leg or ham wound. At other times, the deer may not show any indication at all that it has been hit.

Most hunters are very excited just after hitting a deer, so they should relax a few minutes before moving around, especially if they are in a tree. An excited hunter can actually hurt himself while in a nervous state. I heard one hunter tell about becoming so excited after shooting a large eight-point buck that he jumped up from his seat and started chasing the deer immediately—the only problem being that he was 12 feet up in a tree at the time. His leg was broken when he hit the ground, so not only did he miss the excitement of trailing and finding his deer but he also was in great pain.

After a short waiting period, the hunter should find the exact spot where the deer was standing when hit, and begin looking for telltale signs. He shouldn't give up even if there is no blood. Sometimes a deer will travel several yards before leaving any blood on the trail even with a fatal hit. That is the reason a hunter should watch the deer until it is lost from sight, because somewhere in that area he will most likely find some sign if the deer was hit.

Follow the general direction the deer took from where it was hit to where it was last seen. Watch the ground very closely for tracks, overturned stones, broken twigs, and blood. Always look for the arrow. Examine the arrow for bits of hair, blood, and other matter that may give a clue as to where it entered the deer and what areas it may have severed. Also, by finding the arrow a hunter can confirm a hit or a miss.

When blood is found, examine it closely, because the condition and amount of blood helps to determine where the arrow was placed and how long the hunter should wait before taking up the trail. If blood is found on both sides of the trail, the arrow has penetrated both sides of the deer.

Light red or pinkish blood spots mixed with bubbles indicates a good lung hit and most often means the deer will be down fairly soon. The deer will usually be dead after 30 minutes, or so weakened from the loss of blood that the hunter will be able to approach close enough for a quick finishing shot.

Bright red blood may mean an artery has been severed. If there are indications that the blood is spurting out, then it is almost always an artery hit and a fatal shot. The hunter should give the deer enough time (about 30 minutes) to lie down and bleed out before trailing it.

Very dark blood in small amounts could mean the liver has been cut. Wait at least 30 minutes before following the trail.

Kidney wounds leave a good blood trail. Most bowhunters agree on a 30-minute waiting period for these shots before following the wounded deer.

Heart shots, although very fatal, do not leave much blood. If the hunter is sure that the arrow cut through the heart, he can follow the deer almost immediately and in most cases find it dead within 100 yards. However, there have been cases where a deer has run farther with its heart shot completely away.

Paunch shots leave blood mixed with a greenish-yellow matter, and sometimes bits of undigested food will be found. In most cases, paunch shots mean that the hunter is in for a long hard trailing job, unless the broadhead also cut one of the arteries that serve the paunch area. Many hunters insist on pursuing a paunch-wounded deer immediately—not fast enough to run the deer completely out of the area, but just enough to keep the deer moving and keep the broadhead cutting. Other hunters contend that if given enough time, the deer will lie down, stiffen, and be unable to run from a trailing hunter, thus making it possible to find and finish it off without any further suffering. The latter suggestion has always worked best for me.

Always search the area where the deer was standing when hit, for bits of hair. Very seldom does a broadhead cut through a deer's body without clipping some hair. The color and texture of the hair differ on various parts of the body. For example, the hair found high on the deer will be coarse and will have very dark tips, hair from the middle of the body is medium brown and does not have dark tips, hair low on the body is short and light in color, and hair found on the underside is white.

Another thing to remember when trailing a wounded deer is that when hurt the deer will very seldom travel uphill, because of the discomfort caused by its wound. Also, check out all water holes in the area. A bleeding deer will become very thirsty due to the loss of body fluids. Some hunters believe that a deer goes to water to soothe its wounds. Regardless of why they go, check out the water holes anyway.

If at all possible, solicit the aid of other hunters to help trail a wounded deer, since it is easier to follow a trail when several sets of eyes are searching. Only one or two trackers at a time should follow the trail, to minimize the possibility of disturbing any signs left by the deer. Often the trail has to be rechecked, and destroyed sign cannot be replaced. When sign is found, it should be marked with plainly visible markers. After several markers have been set up, it is sometimes possible to determine where the deer may be heading by the route it is taking. One or two hunters should continue to follow the trail, and a couple of others should check out possible locations where the deer may be.

When a trail is lost, mark the last sign and begin working in semicircles, gradually increasing in size until it is found again. Trail slowly and watch in front of you, because a wounded deer that is not dead can still manage to slip away if it sees the hunter coming, thus making the trailing time that much longer.

Many times a deer is shot in the afternoon and is not found before dark, but if the trackers have good lanterns, the trail will be visible at night. If the trackers have to wait until the next day, the trail will be harder to follow since the blood will dry out to some extent during the night and will not show up too well on the dry winter ground. Also, there is always the possibility that overnight rain will wash away all of the blood. Before trailing at night with a light, be sure to check with the local game department, because it may be illegal to be in the woods with a light after dark.

The beginning bowhunter may find trailing a wounded deer very difficult, and if at all possible he should have an experienced tracker help him until he learns what to look for.

In some states trail dogs are legal and help to find many wounded deer that would otherwise be lost. Here again, the hunter should check the law first, because in some areas it is illegal to have a deer dog in the woods.

The important thing is to follow up every wounded deer until it is found or until it is absolutely impossible to follow it any farther. This will result in more meat in the freezer, less wasted deer, and an overall feeling of a job well done.

FIELD-DRESSING

If you have been successful in tracking your deer and have found it, approach it slowly with an arrow nocked and ready, just in case the deer is not dead. Many hunters have been embarrassed or hurt by hurrying up to a seemingly dead deer, only to have it jump up and either bolt off into the brush or injure the hunter with its sharp hooves. Carefully position yourself so you can see the deer's eyes. If they are glazed over, the deer is probably dead. But it's a good idea to hold your bow ready with one hand and use a long stick to poke the deer until you are assured that it is dead.

If the eyes are not glazed, or if there is any movement when the deer is touched with the stick, do not hesitate to put another arrow into it. Try to place the arrow down through the back of the neck, breaking the spinal column and cutting the large neck arteries. The deer will not go anywhere then, and there should be enough bleeding to make cutting the throat unnecessary.

Many hunters feel that before a deer can be field-dressed, it must have its throat cut so that it can "bleed out." If the deer is going to be field-dressed immediately, as it should be, cutting the throat is not necessary, because all arteries are going to be severed when the internal organs are removed, and most of the blood in the body will drain out at that time. Also, a ragged job of cutting the throat can ruin the cape and make it difficult for the taxidermist, if the head is to be mounted.

When you are sure that the deer is dead, begin field-dressing. Lay the deer on its back and prop it up with rocks or small logs. If you are lucky enough to have someone with you, one of you can hold the deer in place while the other does the dressing.

Force the animal's rear legs apart by placing your knees between them and applying outward pressure. Remove the deer's genitals (or bag if it is a doe) by grasping them firmly with one hand and pulling up, while using a sharp knife to slice the skin away from the body in front of the organs. Cut back toward the pelvic area and the anal vent, deep enough to free the organs at the point where they are attached to the body, but not deep enough to puncture the intestines. Free the anal vent and colon by carefully cutting completely around the vent. When the vent and colon are released, you can pull the lower intestine out of the body far enough to tie it off with a piece of cord, preventing any excrement from spilling into the body cavity as you complete the field-dressing.

133

The Kill

Steps in field-dressing a deer.

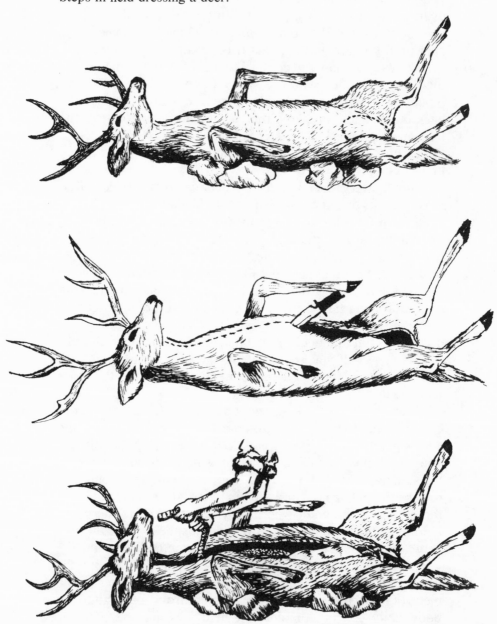

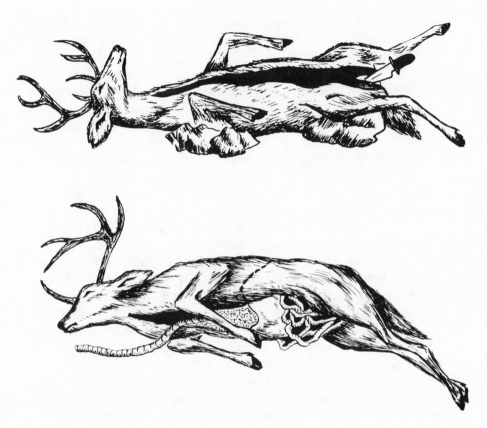

To open the body cavity, begin between the legs by inserting the knife blade under the skin and stomach muscles (cutting edge up). With the fingers of your free hand, keep the internal organs pushed down and the skin pulled up as you make a cut all the way to the jaw. If you are going to save the head for mounting, make sure that you do not cut through the skin on the underside of the neck.

A thin fleshy wall (diaphragm membrane) separates the intestinal cavity and the heart-lung cavity. Cut completely around this membrane, freeing it from the walls of the body. Then reach as far up the inside of the neck as possible and slice through the windpipe and gullet. With a hard downward pull, the windpipe, heart, and lungs can be stripped out to the intestinal cavity. If you like liver and heart, cut them out and save them.

Return to the pelvic area to remove the lower intestines (which were tied off outside the body with a cord at the beginning of the field-dressing) and the sex organs. Slice through the meat to the pelvic bone suture located in the center of the pelvic bone. With the edge of your knife, open the suture separating the bone. A few taps with a rock or stick on the back side of the knife may be required to open the suture.

All of the internal organs are now free from the body cavity, and by rolling the deer on its belly or side they can be removed. Wipe out the body cavity with a rag and prop it open with a short stick to help cool the meat and aid draining.

After you have completed the field-dressing, cut off the small metatarsal glands that are located below midpoint of the lower part of the back legs. If you cut the glands off before field-dressing, be sure not to get any of the musk on your knife or your hands because it may get on the meat and give it a bad taste when it is cooked. Some hunters contend that there is no need to remove the glands at all, but to be on the safe side, remove them. It only takes a few seconds and may mean the difference between a tasty meal and spoiled meat.

If you are not able to put the deer in a cooler immediately, cover it with a game bag to keep flies away, and hang it in the coolest spot available until you are ready to finish preparing it for the freezer.

PACKING OUT

Some hunters are lucky enough to kill their deer in an area where a vehicle can be driven up fairly close in order to pack the meat back to camp. However, in most cases, the deer has to be carried out by manpower and this can present quite a problem, especially if the hunter is alone.

The lone hunter should first field-dress the deer and cover it with a game bag, then hang it up either from a tree or on a tripod, so any remaining blood will drain out. It will also be out of reach of animals. The hunter should then go for help. It is always easier for two or more people to get a deer out of the woods than for a lone hunter to attempt it by himself.

There are several good methods for transporting a deer. A carrying pole is one of the most popular methods used by two hunters. A pole should be selected that is strong yet not too large in diameter, since the weight of the pole itself could become a burden if it is too heavy. Tie the deer's front legs together and the back legs together at the hocks, then slip the pole through the two loops formed by the legs. The pole can now be carried on the shoulders of the two hunters and the weight of the deer will be distributed between the two of them. It is always a good idea to tie the head of the deer firmly to the front legs or to the pole to prevent it from bobbing as the hunters walk. After a few steps, the hunters will realize that by walking "in step" their load will not swing as much, and carrying it will be much easier.

If the deer is a buck, another good way to pack it out is to tie a stick to the antlers. This forms a handle and each hunter will have a firm handhold for pulling his load. For short hauls, some hunters just drag the deer by its antlers.

Another good dragging method, especially if a hunter is alone, is to tie a belt or length of rope around the deer's head and around the hunter's waist or shoulders. Then by simply walking, the deer can be dragged out of the woods.

Never drag a deer by its hind legs after it has been field-dressed, because more dirt and leaves will be shoved into the cavity than if it is dragged by the front legs or head.

If the deer is not too large, a single hunter can carry it out on his shoulders by one of two methods: the one-shoulder carry and the two-shoulder carry.

For the one-shoulder carry, tie all four feet of the deer together and lash the head down firmly to them. The hunter can then put the body of the deer on his shoulder with the feet down or put the feet over his shoulder with the body down. The body-on-the-shoulder method is the most comfortable for long distances.

For the two-shoulder carry, tie the front feet and back feet separately, with the head tied to the front legs. Place the body of the deer across both shoulders with the legs hanging in front of the hunter's body. He can then use the legs for handholds.

A red rag or shirt should always be tied to the antlers of the deer when it is being packed out to prevent some careless hunter from taking a shot at the deer and possibly hitting the person carrying it. Don't laugh, it has happened.

SKINNING

Skinning a deer is not a difficult task, and with a sharp knife it can be accomplished in about five or 10 minutes by following a few simple steps.

1. After the deer has been field-dressed, hang it up by the antlers or neck if the head is not to be mounted (Fig. 1).
2. Cut off the hind legs just below the hocks and the front legs at the knee joint.
3. Cut down the inside of each leg to the belly cut, which was made when the deer was field-dressed.
4. Cut completely around the neck as close to the head as possible.
5. After all of the cuts have been made, grasp the skin with both hands at the neck cut and peel the skin off with a hard downward pull.
6. Use the knife to cut away the skin where it clings to the meat, especially around the legs.
7. Continue pulling and cutting until the skin comes off at the hind legs.
8. After the skin has been removed, hang the deer upside down so all remaining blood and body fluids will drain out (Fig. 2).

Be sure to cover the skinned deer with a game bag to help keep flies away until the deer has cooled and is ready to be butchered.

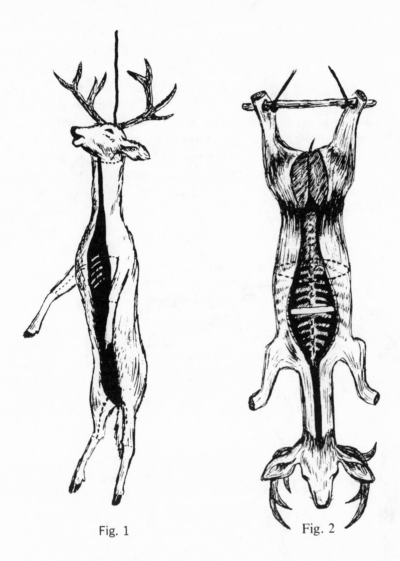

Fig. 1   Fig. 2

Two ways deer can be hung.

If the head is to be mounted, hang the deer by the hind legs instead of the antlers and skin it toward the head. Also, do not cut the brisket any farther than the top of the breastbone, and do not cut around the neck. These cuts make it difficult for a taxidermist to do a good job of mounting. When the skin has been peeled down to the head, do not attempt to skin out the head, just cut it off and take it to the taxidermist with all of the skin attached.

An easy way to skin the deer is to use an automobile to do the pulling after all of the initial cuts have been made. Follow the above steps through number 5, then peel enough of the skin back at the neck to tie a large rock onto it with a strong rope (see illustration). Tie the loose end of the rope to an automobile bumper. Slowly move the auto forward and the skin will be peeled off with a minimum of knife work around tight places.

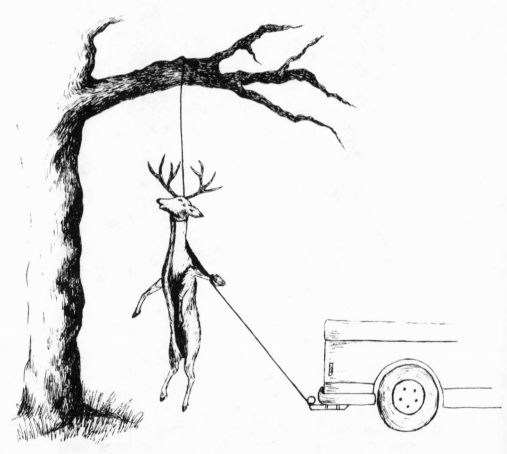

The use of an automobile can be of great assistance in preparing a deer for skinning.

BUTCHERING

So the bowhunter has killed a whitetail, skinned it, and brought it home! What now? The only thing left to do is to get it into the freezer. Many hunters choose to take their deer to a processing plant and let professional butchers cut it for them. Most processing plants will cut the meat to the customer's specifications, wrap and freeze it. For example, my family enjoys deer steak and sausage, so when I use a processing plant I specify that most of the meat be cut into steaks and sausage with maybe one or two good roasts.

When the deer is small, I prefer to do my own butchering. A lot of skill isn't required to do a fairly good job of butchering a deer. A couple of sharp knives and a bone saw or axe are all the tools needed.

Find a good sturdy table and lay the skinned deer on it. Do not use the kitchen table since a missed stroke with the knife can mar a nice table. Remove the front and hind legs, if this has not already been done, by sawing through the bone just above the knees. The portions of meat that were damaged by the arrow should be trimmed away and discarded at this time.

The shoulders will come off easily by cutting with a sharp knife as shown by the dotted line in the diagram. These can either be cut up for roasts, ground for hamburger and sausage, or sliced for fried meat.

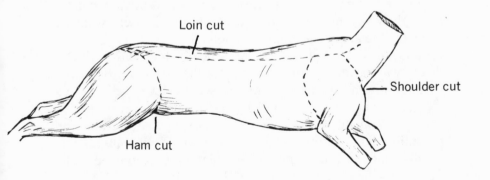

Loin cut

Shoulder cut

Ham cut

The hindquarters are easily removed by cutting through the flank and along the backbone to the ball-and-socket joint, which can be cut through with a saw or knife. The hams will then come off in one big piece. Like the shoulders, the hams can be cut up for roasts, hamburgers, sausages, or fried meat.

Next remove the loins from the top and underside of the backbone by making a long cut along the entire length of the backbone, then make an intersecting cut from the side up the entire length of the backbone. The loin can be lifted off the bone in one long strip, using a knife to cut away places where the two long cuts failed to cross. The loin is the best part of the deer, and when cut into small slices makes delicious fried meat.

All that will be left at this point are the ribs, flanks, and neck. Unless the hunter likes neck roast, the meat can be cut into chunks for stew or ground for hamburger and sausage. The flanks are ground and the ribs chopped up for barbecue or trimmed for ground meat.

After all of the cuts have been made, double wrap the pieces with freezer paper into meal-sized portions, label them and put them in the freezer. Wash the knives, saw, and table, and the job is finished.

MOUNTING THE ANTLERS

The first buck taken with a bow and arrow always means more than any that may follow. Most bowhunters want to have the head or the antlers mounted, but many of them cannot afford a taxidermist. As a result, they either throw them away or attempt to mount them the best way they can. Usually this ends up as a smelly mess and a destroyed trophy.

Several years ago, a good friend of mine, C. L. "Mac" McCarty, taught me an easy and inexpensive method for mounting deer antlers using a plastic-type body putty, with results that are not an embarrassment to hang on the wall. The following sequence explains that method.

Mounting the Antlers

STEP 1. After the deer has been butchered and stored in the freezer, saw the antlers from the head. *Do not attempt to chop them off with an axe.* With one miss-lick, the trophy can very easily be destroyed by breaking the tines with an axe. Start sawing as close behind the antlers as possible without damaging the knurls at the base of each antler. Angle the cut down toward the eyes. When the cut reaches the eye sockets, remove the saw and make an intersecting cut across the face at the eye sockets. The antlers will come off the head when the two cuts meet, leaving enough bone to hold them together. After the antlers have been removed, a sharp knife should be used to cut away as much of the remaining scalp and meat as possible. This is not a pleasant job, because it is very messy, but it must be done if the antlers are to be mounted.

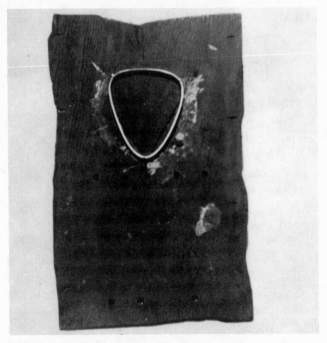

This mold, from the top of a one-pound coffee can, is used when mounting antlers.

STEP 2. Fill an old bucket, pan, or can with enough water to cover the scalp when the antlers are placed inside. Place the container on a stove and bring the water to a boil. The remaining meat is now going to be cooked off the skull. After the antlers have been in the boiling water for several minutes, the meat and hair can be scraped away easily, leaving only the antlers and the bone that connects them. While the antlers are in the boiling water, the bone will often separate at the seam that runs across the top of the skull. Don't worry about this, because a little epoxy will make them good as new.

STEP 3. When all of the hair and meat has been removed, the antlers are ready to be mounted. A mold must be built in order to form the body putty into the desired shape. I usually cut out the lip of the plastic top from a one-pound coffee can and tack it to a board in the shape of a heart (see photo). After the mold has been tacked securely to the board, place the antlers inside the mold and attach them to the board with nails or screws, so they will not move when the putty is applied.

STEP 4. Mix the putty as indicated by the directions on the container, and pour it over the bone portion of the antlers and into the mold. Use a putty knife to push it back into holes and other places where it does not flow. Once the putty has been mixed, it must be used immediately; otherwise it will harden within a few minutes. Be sure to clean the tools used before the mixture hardens on them. Also, clean off any putty that may have gotten on the antlers.

STEP 5. It is difficult to estimate the exact amount of mixture needed to complete the job, so a second batch may be needed. If so, wait until the first application has hardened (preferably the next day) before making the second application. When the second coat of putty is poured, be sure to fill up all holes and smooth it out as much as possible to cut down on the amount of trimming necessary for shaping the mount.

STEP 6. After the putty has hardened, the mount can be shaped with a coarse rasp, then smoothed out with sandpaper. If the mount is to be painted rather than covered with cloth, it must be sanded very smooth. Otherwise, it will show rough

Mounting the Antlers

Applying the putty.

spots after the paint has dried. (*Note:* For the best painting results, use a high-gloss enamel in any desired color. I recommend brown or gray.)

STEP 7. Once the mount has been painted or covered with cloth, the only step left is to place it on a board. Mounting boards can be found in hobby shops, or can be cut out by the hunter himself if he so desires. Varnish the board and drill two or three holes as shown in the photo. Drill matching holes in the back of the mount, and use screws to secure the antlers to the board. Put an eye screw in the top of the board for hanging. The hunter now has a beautiful trophy to remind him of his successful hunt for years to come.

A mounting board showing location of the holes.

PART VI

OTHER POINTS
OF INTEREST

FAMILY-STYLE HUNTING

A few years ago hunting and camping were considered to be strictly male activities. Each time hunting season rolled around wives all over the country would become "weekend widows." They would stay at home while their men took to the woods. Not so anymore!

Along with the commercialization of camping and the introduction of all types of conveniences for making camp life easier, women began to develop an interest in hunting and camping. Once they started camping they enjoyed it, and now many women look forward to deer season as much if not more than their men.

My wife had never camped or hunted until a few years ago, but now she loves it. I talked her into going with me one weekend to check out a deer lease where several families would be bowhunting together that fall. She was not particularly interested in sleeping in the back of our truck or eating my cooking—she had refused to do the cooking on a camp fire—but she finally agreed to go.

When we arrived at the camp site, she stepped out of the truck, took a long look around and asked, "Where is the rest room?" I told her that she was standing in the middle of about 600 acres of it. That must have broken the ice, because after that she took to camp life like she had been doing it for years. Since that time, she has even taken up bowhunting and sits in her tree right along with the rest of us. However, when we returned home after that first weekend she bought us a camper and a portable toilet.

There is no reason why the whole family cannot enjoy hunting. My family is one of a group that gets together each year with campers, bows, and kids, and heads for the deer woods for a couple of weeks. The children love it because of the freedom to run, jump, and play to their hearts' content. The women love it because there are no daily chores and errands to run. The men love it because their wives no longer complain about being left at home while they go off to the woods and have a good time. Many of the women in our group have killed as many deer as the men.

When most men, myself included, go to the deer woods they take only the bare necessities: something to eat, something to cover up with at night, and something to hunt with. That is what is referred to as "roughing it." But when the whole family goes, a few other items usually must be taken along. There is so much camping equipment offered on today's market that to mention it all would take a catalog.

Before visiting a sporting-goods store to pick out what he needs, a beginner should talk with an experienced camper and get his help in making a list of needed items. Otherwise, he may leave the store with a truck load of equipment that will never be used.

Some serious hunters still think that a hunting trip is not the place for women and children, that "they will scare the deer." This is not true unless the lease is either very small or the children are allowed to play all over it. Our group uses approximately 10 acres for camping and a playground. The rest of the lease is undisturbed except for the hunters.

We are all tree sitters, so most of our hunting is done in the early morning and late afternoon. Long before daybreak, we are on our way to the trees where we stay until around 10:00 A.M. During the day, we eat, sleep, read, talk, play cards, or trail deer that were hit during the morning hunt. Then around 3:30 P.M. everyone starts getting ready for the afternoon hunt. By 4:30 P.M. we are back in our trees where we stay until dark.

Our group probably does waste several hunting hours a day by not stalking during the period between the morning and afternoon hunts, but that is the way we like it. Other groups can work out their own schedules.

SAFETY

Personal safety as well as the safety of other hunters should always be in the mind of every hunter. No one really thinks

Family practice time.

that he will get hurt or hurt someone else, but it does happen. Each year there are numerous accounts of hunter accidents, many that could have been avoided by taking a few safety precautions.

Bowhunting is not as dangerous as gun hunting in the respect of shooting someone else, since the range of the weapon is much shorter, but there have been cases where careless bowhunters shot in the direction of other persons and hit them. The best way to prevent this is to be certain of the target before the arrow is released. Never shoot at movement in the brush, even if a deer has been seen entering the

151

thicket. Many hunters are killed or seriously injured each year because some hunter mistook them for a deer.

Of course, there have been incidents where one hunter shot another by a freak accident that could not be considered carelessness. This happened to my friend Jim Hoedebeck while we were bowhunting for wild hogs on a preserve in east Texas.

Several groups of bowhunters were hunting that day and the hogs were moving everywhere, so we were all getting a lot of action. Jim happened to be walking down an old road toward the area where the automobiles were parked, and another hunter was coming from the parking area toward the hunting area, meeting Jim. There was a deep, almost 45-degree curve between them. As the two hunters approached the curve, neither could see the other. When they were about 25 yards from the curve, a hog spooked and ran across the road at the bend. Both hunters saw it and shot. Jim's arrow flew over the hog's back into the brush. The other hunter's arrow struck a tree at just the right angle to deflect it in Jim's direction. This could only happen once in a million times, but it angled away from the tree at almost 45 degrees and hit Jim in the foot. The wound was not serious, though it did bleed a lot and was very painful.

This type of accident cannot be avoided, since it happens through no carelessness on the hunter's part. However, most accidents can be attributed to carelessness, so it behooves the bowhunter to follow a few "dos and don'ts."

1. Don't shoot at movement. It could have been made by another hunter.
2. Don't shoot an arrow high into the air. It may come down on someone else.
3. Don't walk with a nocked arrow. If you should fall, the broadhead could cut you or someone else.
4. Don't enter camp with a nocked arrow for the same reason as number 3.
5. Don't try to climb a tree with the bow and arrow in your hand. Carry a string and draw them up to you after you are safely seated on a limb.

6. When hunting from a high stand, use a safety belt to prevent a fall.
7. Always carry a first-aid kit.
8. If hunting in an area where poisonous snakes are known to be, carry a snake-bite kit.
9. Never wear shoes or boots that do not fit. They could cause blisters or sore feet, which can ruin a good hunt.
10. Never use broken arrows or arrows that are too short for your draw length. During the excitement of shooting at a deer, you may overdraw and send the arrow through your hand or arm.
11. When hunting in strange areas carry a compass, and watch for landmarks that could lead you back if you become lost.
12. Don't hunt alone if you have a physical condition that could strike at any time.
13. If you are hunting alone, let someone know where you are going and approximately when you will return.
14. If hunting with a group, have a prearranged meeting time and place.
15. If you become lost, do not wander around. Stay where you are and build a fire if possible. The smoke may lead others to your position.
16. If you build a fire, be sure to keep it under control and put it out before leaving.
17. Get into good condition before the season begins.

GETTING INTO SHAPE FOR HUNTING

Getting the body in shape for hunting is as important to hunter safety as any other thing, because a body that is in poor condition cannot take a vigorous hunting trip and often the hunter ends up being hunted by his companions. Heart attacks and exhaustion are not uncommon on hunting trips, even with people who seem to be in perfect health before the hunt begins.

Too many of us living in the modern world fail to realize just how little exercise we get each day. The muscles that are used daily are not the ones needed when following a deer trail. So a hunter must exercise on a regular basis for several weeks before hunting season or the hunt may be ruined by a trip to the hospital. Start by walking every day. A person should not drive anywhere if he can walk instead. At first he may find that his legs become tired after a brisk mile. But after a few days the leg muscles will begin to grow stronger and a second or third mile can be added.

Another good exercise to help build the leg muscles and control breathing is to walk up and down stairs or hills if possible. Do not overdo the exercise at first. Start slowly and work up to longer hikes and steeper hills.

While training for the hunting season, the hunter can also break in his new hunting clothes and boots. The neighbors may think that he has gone out of his mind, but he'll be much better off on opening day.

NFAA AWARD PROGRAM

As mentioned earlier in the guide, the NFAA offers an award program that allows an archer to receive awards for the game that he takes with a bow and arrow. Participation in this program helps to keep the bowhunter's interest up during the off-season and at the same time helps to improve his hunting ability.

The following is a slightly edited excerpt from the NFAA rule book and explains the program.

ARTICLE XVI
ART YOUNG AWARDS

A. Game Awards of the National Field Archery Association

1. There shall be two: the "Art Young Big-Game Awards" and "Art Young Small-Game Awards."
2. Purpose: The purpose of the Art Young awards is to promote interest in hunting with the bow and arrow, to encourage good sportsmanship, and to give recognition by the organized field archers to their members who obtain game with the bow.
3. Rules:
   (a) All animals must be taken in accordance with the laws of the state, territory, province, or county, whichever is appropriate, and in accordance with the rules of fair chase.
   (b) In order to be eligible for awards, all animals must be reported within 90 days of the date taken. A handling fee of 50 cents must accompany each application.
   (c) The hunter must have taken possession of the animal to receive credit for the award.
   (d) It shall be the responsibility of the hunter himself to know the legal status of the species hunted.

National Headquarters is responsible only to the extent of verifying whether a species is or is not protected, since this is the basis of acceptance.

(e) Animals specified as big game by the NFAA are not eligible for credit in the Art Young Small-Game Awards system.

(f) Members who willfully take game out of season, take protected animals or otherwise violate game laws, falsify a claim or deliberately witness a falsified claim shall be expelled from the NFAA and all its programs. An expelled member may petition the NFAA for reinstatement after one year. The Bow-hunting and Conservation Committee shall rule on the petition.

(g) An additional award shall not be given for game previously accepted under a prior awards system. (Persons who have amassed a combination of seven or more pins under the original program as of July 1, 1973, and have so requested by January 1, 1974, shall be allowed to continue the original program. The same animals used in claiming any portion of the original Master Bowhunter Award may not be used again for awards in another program.)

(h) Any game taken from areas where they are officially designated as "rare" or "endangered" shall be ineligible for awards.

B. *Art Young Big-Game Awards*

1. Definition of Big Game:
   (a) All species of American bears. For lack of confusion the "Alaskan brown bear" will be considered a grizzly (now so recognized by most modern taxonomists).

(b) Big cats including mountain lions or cougars.

(c) The deer family including elk, moose, caribou, and various species of native deer.

(d) All other native hoofed animals including pronghorns, sheep, goats, and javelina.

(e) All feral (gone wild) swine (boars), sheep, and goats if recognized as "game" by the local conservation department.

(f) Any animal considered big game by the local county or province.

2. Eligibility: Eligibility for "Art Young Big-Game Awards" is limited to members of the NFAA at the time of the kill. There shall be no geographical restrictions, either as to residence of the claimant or to the location in which the game is secured.

3. Claim of Award: Any member of the NFAA wishing to claim the Art Young Big-Game Pin, or the subsequent awards, will apply to the NFAA Headquarters for an application blank, supply the information and evidence called for, and mail it to NFAA Headquarters.

4. Awards:

(a) Art Young Big-Game Pins shall be given for only the first example of each species taken with the bow and arrow according to the NFAA rules.

(b) Cloth patches for additional examples of each species taken with the bow and arrow according to the NFAA rules will be awarded.

C. *Art Young Small-Game Awards*

1. Definition of Small Game:

(a) Any animal recognized as small game by the local conservation department in the area taken.

(b) Any small mammal, bird, fish, or poisonous reptile generally recognized as a nuisance or harmful, but not necessarily defined as game by law.

2. Eligibility: This shall be the same as for the "Art Young Big-Game Award." If several species are taken within such a 90-day period, they may be held and reported at one time. However, no species may be reported more than 90 days after taking.

3. Awards:
   (a) The Art Young Small-Game Arrowhead Pin shall be given upon taking the first six species of small game.
   (b) For each additional four species taken by a member an additional award in the form of a bar with the number 4 shall be presented to the hunter. There shall be no limit to the number of bars that may be earned, but all game must be legally taken.
   (c) A separate patch shall be made available for each species taken.
   (d) A particular species may not be claimed more than once by any bowhunter participating in the Art Young Small-Game Program, except in states that have fewer than three species designated legal small game for bowhunting. At least one of the animals claimed must be considered "game" by the local conservation department.

D. Bowhunter Awards

1. There shall be three classes of Bowhunter Awards:
   (a) Bowhunter Pin
   (b) Expert Bowhunter Pin
   (c) Master Bowhunter Medal
2. Eligibility:
   (a) A person may be awarded the Bowhunter Pin when he has earned the Art Young Small-Game Arrowhead Pin and one Four bar, and two Big-Game Arrowhead Pins.

(b) A person may be awarded the Expert Bowhunter Pin when he has earned the Bowhunter Pin plus one additional Four bar and one additional Big-Game Arrowhead Pin.

(c) A person may be awarded the Master Bowhunter Medal when he has earned the Expert Bowhunter Pin plus three additional Four bars and three additional Big-Game Arrowhead Pins.

3. Claim of Awards applications must be made to the NFAA Headquarters. Verification that all species, to the best of his knowledge, were legally taken must be made by another NFAA member. No application will be accepted by NFAA without such verification.

E. Diamond Buck Award

1. The Diamond Buck Award will be given for the largest example of mule deer, whitetail deer, and blacktail deer based on antler measurements. The antlers must be scored by Pope and Young Club or Boone and Crockett methods and verified by one of these club's official measurers. Applications shall be available from NFAA Headquarters and from Sectional Officers of the NFAA in charge of bowhunting.

F. Application Disapproval

1. In the event an application is disapproved, the hunter has the right to petition the NFAA Bowhunting and Conservation Committee. The petition must be in writing and must state the facts of the claim. It shall be the responsibility of the review committee to study the applicable game laws and the petition and make a recommendation to the Bowhunting and Conservation Committee. The chairman shall appoint the three-man

committee to rule on the claim and act on the claim within 60 days.
2. The results of the petition shall be kept confidential, but the ruling shall be sent in writing to each member of the committee, the NFAA Headquarters, and the petitioner.

PART VII

RECIPES FOR COOKING VENISON

The meat of the whitetail deer offers some very delicious meals if prepared properly, and the successful hunter should never throw it away or give it to someone else until he has tried venison himself. The following recipes are a few of the favorites of my family. Each recipe will serve five persons.

VENISON PIE

1 pound ground venison
3 cups creamed potatoes
1/2 pound shredded cheddar cheese

Precook ground meat in a small skillet. Prepare creamed potatoes in the usual manner, using either instant or fresh potatoes. Place ground meat in the bottom of a casserole and spread potatoes over it. Add the shredded cheese on top and allow it to melt in a 450-degree preheated oven. When the cheese has melted, the dish is ready to serve.

Serving suggestions: rolls, tossed green salad, and a dessert of your choice.

FRIED VENISON STEAK

1/2 cup flour
1/2 cup meal
1/2 cup instant potato flakes
1 pound thinly sliced steak
1 cup milk

Thoroughly mix flour, meal, and potato flakes into a batter. Use your choice of seasoning on the steaks, then dip them in milk and the batter. Drop them in boiling grease and fry to a golden brown. *Do not overcook.*

Serving suggestions: cream gravy, hot biscuits, and vegetables of your choice.

BARBECUE VENISON

1 pound thinly sliced strips of venison
Barbecue sauce of your choice

Place strips of venison on a hot grill or in an oven broiler and cover them with sauce. Turn often and continue covering them with sauce each time until they are cooked through.

Serving suggestions: tossed green salad and baked beans with hot rolls.

VENISON CHILI

1 pound ground venison
1 pound block of chili
3 cups red (pinto) beans

Lightly brown the ground venison in a small skillet. Prepare chili block and precooked beans in a large saucepan and add browned venison. Allow to simmer for about 30 minutes and serve.

Serving suggestions: crackers, milk, and dessert of your choice.

BARBECUE VENISON HOT LINKS

5 large venison links
Barbecue sauce of your choice
$1/2$ pound shredded cheddar cheese

Split the links and fill with sauce. Cook for approximately 30 minutes in a 400-degree oven. Top with shredded cheese and allow it to melt.

Serving suggestions: tossed salad, green vegetable of your choice, refried beans, and hot rolls.

GLOSSARY
OF ARCHERY
AND
BOWHUNTING
TERMS

Armguard: The protector pad worn on the inside of the bow arm to keep the string from slapping the arm.

Arrow plate: A protector or inlay to protect the bow as the arrow passes by the handle when shot.

Back: The side of the bow facing away from the archer when held in the shooting position.

Backing: The material used on the back of a bow to increase its cast.

Bast: The coiled straw backing of a target on which a target face is attached. Sometimes referred to as "boss."

Blind: Place of concealment for a bowhunter to keep game from seeing him.

Bow shelf: Cutout on bow handle where the arrow lays when ready to be shot. Also called arrow shelf.

Bowyer: One who makes bows.

Brace (v.): To place the string on the bow.

Broadhead: A hunting arrow point.

Butt: A target backstop.

Cant: Angle of bow to right or left of center when in a shooting position.

Cast: The ability of a bow to shoot an arrow.

Cock feather: The feather that is at a right angle to the nock slot.

Draw: Pulling the string back with an arrow in place ready for shooting.

Draw fingers: The fingers used to draw the string.

Draw weight: The energy required to draw a bow to its full position; measured in pounds.

Driving: Pushing game in the direction of standers.

"Expert": A person who has killed at least one whitetail and now knows everything about deer hunting.

Glossary of Archery and Bowhunting Terms

Eye: The loop in each end of a bowstring.

Field point: An arrowhead used for small game.

Fistmele: Brace height of the bowstring; the distance between the bow handle and the string.

Fletch (v.): To attach feathers to an arrow shaft.

Fletching: The feathers on an arrow that serve as a rudder when the arrow is in flight.

Flu-flu: An arrow with extra large fletching used for wing shooting.

Grip or handle: Part of the bow held in the bow hand.

Group: The strike pattern of arrows in a target.

Heeling: Letting the heel of the bow hand apply pressure to the bow handle when in shooting position.

Hen feathers: The feathers that are not at right angles to the nock slot.

Hold: The short pause after full draw is reached, before the arrow is released.

Laminated bow: A bow made with layers of materials glued together.

Limb: Either half of the bow, from the handle to the tip.

Nock: Slotted end of the arrow or the bow where the string fits.

Nocking point: Where the arrow nock fits over the bowstring.

Overdraw: To draw the bow farther than the distance for which it was designed.

Pinch: Squeezing the arrow between the draw fingers.

Pluck (v.): To jerk the string with the draw fingers when the arrow is released.

Pope and Young Club: Similar to the Boone and Crockett Club, but for archers instead of gun hunters.

Quiver: A device designed for carrying extra arrows.

Glossary of Archery and Bowhunting Terms

Recurved bow: A bow where both ends bend away from the archer.

Release: The act of turning the arrow loose.

Serving: The wrapped area of a bowstring to protect the string from wear.

Shaft: The body of an arrow.

Shooting glove: Three-fingered glove used to protect the draw fingers when shooting.

Shot window: Cutout in a bow handle.

Spine: Stiffness of an arrow.

Stacking: The rapid buildup of draw weight as a bow is drawn.

Stalking: Silent approach of deer or other game.

Stand: An area chosen by a hunter where he waits for game.

Stander: One who uses a hunting stand.

Straight bow: A bow where the ends are straight and do not bend away from the archer.

Tab: Finger protector for the draw fingers.

Venison: Deer meat used for food.

INDEX

Index

Boldface numbers refer to illustrations